BRAZIL'S FOLK – POPULAR POETRY
"A LITERATURA DE CORDEL"

A Bilingual Anthology in English and Portuguese

Mark J. Curran

Professor Emeritus
Arizona State University

Order this book online at www.trafford.com
or email orders@trafford.com

Most Trafford titles are also available at major online book retailers.

© Copyright 2010 Mark J. Curran.

All rights reserved. No part of this publication may be reproduced, stored in a retrieval system, or transmitted, in any form or by any means, electronic, mechanical, photocopying, recording, or otherwise, without the written prior permission of the author.

Printed in Victoria, BC, Canada.

ISBN: 978-1-4269-2469-9 (sc)

Library of Congress Control Number: 2010900324

Our mission is to efficiently provide the world's finest, most comprehensive book publishing service, enabling every author to experience success. To find out how to publish your book, your way, and have it available worldwide, visit us online at www.trafford.com

Trafford rev. 03/02/2010

 www.trafford.com

North America & international
toll-free: 1 888 232 4444 (USA & Canada)
phone: 250 383 6864 • fax: 812 355 4082

Table of Contents

Introduction — 1

The Story - Poems of "Cordel" — 25

1. — 27
"Debate of the Protestant Preacher with Master Vulture"
"Debate d'um Ministro Nova-Seita e Urubú"
Attributed to Leando Gomes de Barros

2. — 37
"Money"
"O Dinheiro"
Leandro Gomes de Barros

3. — 47
"The Girl Who Beat Up Her Mother and Was Turned into a Dog"
"A Moça que Bateu na Mãe e Virou Cachorra"
Rodolfo Coelho Cavalcante

4. — 59
"Story of Mariquinha and José de Sousa Leão"
"História de Mariquinha e José de Sousa Leão"
João Ferreira de Lima

5. — 83
"Sufferings of the Northeasterner Traveling to the South"
"Os Martírios do Nortista Viajando para o Sul"
Cícero Vieira da Silva, "Mocó"

6. — 95
"Poetic Duel between Patrick and Ignatius from Catingueira"
"Peleja de Patrício e Inácio da Catingueira"
Attributed to Joao Martins de Atayde

7.   105

"The Encounter of Tancredo with St. Peter in Heaven"
"O Encontro de Tancredo com São Pedro no Céu"
Chiquinho do Pandeiro and Master Azulão

8.   119

"The End of the War and the Death of Hitler and Mussolini"
"O Fim da Guerra e a Morte de HITLER e MUSSOLINE"
Delarme Monteiro da Silva

9.   129

"Debate between Lampião and an American Tourist"
"Debate de Lampião com a Turista Americana"
Franklin Maxado Nordestino

10.   141

"Trip to St. Saruê"
"Viagem a São Saruê"
Manoel Camilo dos Santos

Bibliography of Secondary Works on "Cordel"   151

Introduction[1]

The folk-popular poetry, or so-called "string literature" [literatura de cordel] of northeastern Brazil, is basically a hybrid literature of both popular and folkloric forms. The poetry is "popular" in the strict sense because the author is generally known and his name appears on the cover and first page of the booklet of verse [folheto, romance], and the poetry is printed in booklets on inexpensive paper, originally a modest quality of newsprint, and sold in the plazas, markets and street corners of many towns and cities of Brazil.[2] On the other hand, the roots of "cordel" are from the folk tradition: many of its themes, metrical forms, and its performance come from the oral tradition of Brazil's northeast. Thus the cordelian poet [o poeta popular de feira] has a lot in common with the northeastern troubadour or poet-singer [o cantador] who improvises and "sings" the poetry. The latter either "sings" or declaims improvised poetry in the markets or fairs in a poetic duel, accompanied by a partner or rival, the duel being an extremely ancient phenomenon from the western poetic tradition.

There was a type of poetic tradition akin to "cordel" that existed in Brazil on a small scale as early as the 16th and 17th centuries, but it

---

1 In this introduction to the bilingual anthology of the folk-popular poetry of Brazil, the text will be in English and terms in Portuguese will be enclosed in brackets, i.e. folk-popular literature [literatura de cordel].
2 Our explanation of the "cordel" is in the present tense and depicts the reality of the poetry as it existed throughout most of the 20th century. Many changes have taken place since and will be noted as we proceed to tell the story.

took a different form than "cordel" in its heyday in the 19th and 20th centuries. This earlier tradition was probably first seen in single pages of printed verse, a sort of "poetic flyer" [volante] brought to Brazil and enjoyed by the Portuguese colonizers. But "cordel's" definitive Brazilian form dates from the end of the 19th century in the northeastern part of the country.

Among the first known booklets of verse [folhetos de feira] were those imported to Brazil from Portugal by the Garnier Bookstore in Rio de Janeiro at the end of the 19th century. The popular stories contained in these booklets were brought to the Northeast where they took root, grew and were eventually converted into what would become a vibrant northeastern and Brazilian tradition. The evolution of this folk-popular poetry is a long and complicated matter; in this book our goal is to simply provide the basics of that story. The original booklets imported by Garnier were generally in prose; the poets of the Northeast transcribed the stories in prose to verse, generally in strophes of six or seven lines with eight syllables in each line, coincidentally the length of the most famous metric form in Spain and Portugal -- the romance [romance]. Rhyme schemes were therefore either abcbdb or ababccb with both vowels and consonants rhyming from the last accented syllable.

The body of subject matter, themes and stories comes from popular Iberian tradition, principally Portuguese, but also Spanish, and other European and even Mid -- Eastern sources. This corpus was adapted and recreated and would eventually be replaced by what was no less than a portrait of life and reality in northeastern Brazil.[3] The beauty and charm of the Brazilian "cordel" is that even today, the beginnings of the 21st century, its traditional themes continue alive in Brazil, this in spite of all the pressures of modern life, although its form and content have changed to adapt to the times.[4]

3   Consult Gustavo Barroso, Ao Som da Viola (Rio de Janeiro: Departamento de Imprensa Nacional, 1949).
4   The arrival of the P.C. and a printer at its side has changed "cordel" significantly. Most poets today write their story on the computer and print the "folhetos" one at a time on the printer. The poetry takes the same form as described, although topics may be contemporary; the woodcut is still used to illustrate many of the covers of the booklets of verse, but the paper is generally of much higher quality

The term "literatura de cordel" or "string literature" is relatively new in Brazil and is the result of scholars writing about it and basing the term on the tradition and terminology of an ancestral phenomenon in Portugal. Luís da Câmara Cascudo, the dean of Brazilian folklorists, traces the name to the Portuguese "literatura de cordel" which was sold with the booklet draped over a string or wire in the market stall. The literature was also known as "blind men's literature" due to the fact that blind men were common sellers of the verse.[5] But the booklets in verse were known in Brazil throughout the 20th century by various other names by the people that composed, printed, read and sold them: "folhetos, folhetes, folhetos de feira, histórias, ABCs," and in the Golden Age of "cordel", "arrecifes" or "reefs" -- a term which refers to the production of story-poems in the city of Recife, Pernambuco, located on the ocean on the Atlantic coast, by the poet and publisher João Martins de Atayde from the 1930s to the late 1950s.

It is an extremely difficult task to identify the definitive European origins of the original body or corpus of "cordel." There are many studies from the masters which treat the matter: once again, Câmara Cascudo's work in the 1950s, our own in brief fashion in 1973, and more recently, Candace Slater.[6] What is certain is that the roots of Brazilian "cordel" are much more closely related to written, popular literature in Iberia than the oral or even written tradition of the Iberian "romances" [romances]. However, Ariano Suassuna, fan and one of the masters of the matter in Brazil, likes to use the term "romanceiro popular nordestino" when referring to the "cordel".[7] Thus it helps to

> than the old news print. Many young poets use these techniques and a few of the old timers as well. Another change relates to social class: many current day poets come from Brazil's middle class, a definite change from the old days. And there is an all together different phenomenon -- "cordel" on the internet -- an amazingly vibrant tradition today but missing many of the "traditional" traits of cordel in print.

5 See Luís da Câmara Cascudo, Cinco Livros do Povo (Rio de Janeiro: José Olympio, 1953).
6 Slater's book is the definitive study on "cordel" in English. See Candace Slater, Stories on a String: the Brazilian "Literatura de Cordel" (Berkeley: the University of California Press, 1982).
7 Ariano Suassuna, "A Compadecida e o Romanceiro Nordestino," Literatura Popular em Verso: Estudos, t. 1 (Rio de Janeiro: Ministério de Educação – Fundação Casa de Rui Barbosa, 1973).

be familiar with the tradition of the "chapbooks" or "broadsides" in England, the "littérature de colportage" in France, the "pliegos sueltos" and "literatura de cordel" in Spain, and, finally, "blind man's literature" [a literatura dos cegos] of the 16th and 17th centuries in Portugal. All these popular literatures, until recently little appreciated in Western erudite tradition, have their differences and their similarities, and variations of them were brought to the New World where they existed isolated from each other from the end of one continent to the end of the other until folklorists in the 20th century began to create interest in the phenomenon.[8]

Brazilian "cordel," specifically, has survived in spectacular and important form in Brazilian cultural life. Without doubt, those readers familiar with the Argentine poetic duel [la payada argentina], the Mexican song-ballads [los corridos mexicanos], and especially the corpus of folk stories from various countries that deal with fairies, princes, monsters, saints and events or beings "never seen before," will appreciate this tradition so rooted in the popular life of a neighboring country.

No one knows for certain who wrote the first booklet of "cordel" native to Brazil, but there are sporadic verses printed in booklets about the War of Canudos in 1896.[9] A little later, the Paraiban poet Silvino Piraúa Lima published his poetry in the cordelian format. But the first great name of Brazilian "cordel" and still of greatest renown today is Leandro Gomes de Barros who wrote and published his works on the outskirts of the northeastern city of Recife, Pernambuco, from the end of the 19th century to the teens of the 20th. It should be noted also that Leandro Gomes de Barros was from the State of Paraíba, from which came the majority of the great names in the oral, folkloric poetry, that is, of the poet-singers [cantadores] of northeastern Brazil. It is surmised that Gomes de Barros wrote and published perhaps up to one thousand poems in a career lasting more than twenty years, several of the poems

---

8 See Vicente Mendoza, El Romance Español y el Corrido Mexicano (México: Imprenta Universitaria, 1939) and Merle Simmons, The Mexican 'Corrido' as a Source for the Interpretive Study of Modern Mexico (Bloomington: Indiana University Press, 1957).

9 See José Calasans, O Ciclo Folclórico do Bom Jesus Conselheiro (Salvador: Tipografia Beneditina Ltda., 1950).

becoming "classics" in the genre.[10] He was known especially for the humorous and satiric tone of his verse about the Brazilian political, economic and social reality, but he also was the creator of wonderful "traditional romances," [romances tradicionais], that is, long narrative poems with traditional Brazilian-European themes.

After the 1920s and the end of Leandro Gomes de Barros' career, but with the visibility and fame of "cordel" on the rise, the "trade" or vocation of cordelian poet and publisher became semi-professionalized. The great "impresario" of "cordel," João Martins de Atayde, wrote and published hundreds of titles printed in Recife, Pernambuco, but distributed and sold the story-poems in all the Northeast and North of Brazil. He was followed by other poet-publishers like José Bernardo da Silva in Juazeiro do Norte, Ceará; Manoel Camilo dos Santos in Guarabira, Paraíba; João José da Silva in Recife; Manoel D'Almeida Filho in Aracaju, Sergipe; Cuíca de Santo Amaro and Rodolfo Coelho Cavalcante in Salvador da Bahia, and many others. Thus "cordel" was written and published in all the states of the Brazilian Northeast.

With the internal migratory movements in Brazil at the end of the 19th and beginning of the 20th centuries, the folk-popular poetry [cordel] of the Northeast moved with the poets who accompanied this phase of Brazilian life. With the rubber boom in the Amazon basin at the beginning of the 20th century, the waves of northeastern migrants to the rich southeast cities of São Paulo and Rio de Janeiro and adjacent farm areas, and the construction of the new capital Brasília in the center of the country in the 1950s, "cordel" geographically augmented its market. When this author began studies of "cordel" in the 1960s, it was necessary to travel from São Paulo and Rio de Janeiro in the south-southeast, through the Valley of the São Francisco River in Minas Gerais and the backlands of the State of Bahia, through all the Northeast, the birthplace of "cordel," and as far as the Amazon region to collect story-poems and interview poets.

---

10 Câmara Cascudo, <u>Cinco Livros do Povo</u>, p. 12. There are scholars who doubt such a high number, but no one doubts the importance and quality of his total work.

The 1970s and 1980s brought change to the country and as well to the writers, publishers and public of "cordel." The enemies of the poor masses -- monetary inflation, the resulting high cost of living, in short, the economic crisis of the country -- affected the poets who wrote and printed their verse to be sold to a humble public. The sales of "cordel" fell significantly; the buying public no longer had the resources to buy the booklets of "cordel," in an ever upward spiral in price.[11] In addition, the poet no longer had the means to pay to publish his story-poem in the local typography; the price of ink and paper had spiraled as well. Another factor closely related to the change was the beginning of the gradual decrease or even disappearance of the local weekly fairs in the small towns of the Northeast, "cordel's" primary place of sale.

There were other important factors: the country was rapidly modernizing; roads, highways and transport increased at breakneck speed; the transistor radio arrived at a price available to the most humble citizen; and suddenly television and then color television appeared on the scene. In short, Brazil, including its poorest area in the Northeast, and the greater part of the potential market for "cordel," began to confront life in the modern 20th century. Migration to the city, mass media and basically a change in taste were factors as well in the diminished "cordel."

The results, in general, were not happy for "cordel." The traditional public of the humble class disappeared little by little for various reasons both economic and social. The "masters" of the heyday of "cordel" grew old or died, and others were forced to search out new ways to make a living. The result was that "cordel" diminished rapidly and significantly as poetry written for and sold to the humble class both in the tiny towns of the northeastern interior and its large coastal cities.

But it is also true that a new public emerged as potential buyers of "cordel" during this period of the 1970s and 1980s: intellectuals, artists,

---

11 One can trace the cost of living and inflation of the Brazilian economy through the changes in price of the booklet of cordelian verse – from the "mil-réis" of the teens of the 20th century to the "cruzeiro" of the 1960s, to the "new cruzeiro" of the late 1960s, the "cruzado" and finally to the "real" of recent years. Booklets of verse which cost five cents in U.S. money in the 1960s today cost fifty cents in the same currency. This 1000 per cent increase in cost reflects as well the general cost of living in Brazil.

students from the middle class, and avid tourists curious about "Brazilian folklore."[12] With the aforementioned new public and the same public of humble class with northeastern roots, the latter "new" migrants to São Paulo and Rio de Janeiro, the buying public for "cordel" was no longer homogeneous, but really pluralist. And, as to be expected, "cordel" changed as well. The liveliest place to find "cordel" in the late 1970s was the northeastern market in the north zone of Rio de Janeiro! And a significant public was to be found in São Paulo as well, particularly in the "Plaza of the Republic" [Praça de República] in downtown São Paulo on Sunday mornings. The old "Mecca" of "cordel," Recife, lessened in importance and in fact was almost devoid of "cordel" for a few years in the late 1970s. And while this happened, the traditional buyers of "cordel" diminished. Even worse, the "cordel" that had gained new interest by middle and even upper class curiosity seekers in a sort of "fad" of discovering folk-popular culture in Rio or São Paulo or tourist trips to the Northeast, eventually diminished as well.

Yet, as of today's writing in 2009, as mentioned earlier in the notes, there have been significant changes to the situation just described of the 1970s and 1980s. There are really two phenomena taking place: the first a resurgence in "traditional" "cordel" in its written form, the booklets of verse of eight or more pages, the second, "cordel" on the internet.

Today there are many young writers of "traditional" "cordel," often from the middle class; in addition, there are a few old-timers in the Northeast like the beloved veteran José Costa Leite of Condado, Pernambuco, and Abraão Batista of Juazeiro do Norte and J. Borges of Pernambuco who continue to write and sell their poems. Second generation writers, like Marcelo Soares, the very successful son of the old "cordelian reporter," José Soares, are active as well. Azulão continues in greater Rio as does Gonçalo Ferreira da Silva with his "Brazilian Academy of 'Literatura de Cordel'" in the Santa Teresa section of Rio in the former center founded by the late Umberto Peregrino, "Casa de São Saruê." There are in addition many authors this writer has not personally met. What is significant, by and large, is the <u>reason</u> for this resurgence.

---

12 See Mark J Curran, "Brazil's 'Literatura de Cordel': Its Distribution and Adaptation to the Brazilian Mass Market." <u>Studies in Latin American Popular Culture</u>, I, (1982): 164-178.

It boils down to the use of the personal computer with printer at its side to write and print story-poems still in the format of traditional "cordel," i.e. 4 X 6 inches, on good quality paper and with a colored cover often using the traditional northeastern woodcut as cover decoration.

The computer-copier-printer combination enables current poets to print story-poems in fairly large printings over a period of time. What also is significant (information garnered from poets at the "International Congress of Literatura de Cordel" in João Pessoa in 2005 with a significant "cordel fair" at its side) is the ever increasing access these poets have to grade school, high school and even university classrooms to recite and sell their story-poems.

An entirely different phenomenon is "cordel" on the internet. There are dozens of web pages available. One of the most prominent is that of Gustavo Dourado of Brasília. Note that a certain amount of self-promotion has always been necessary to survive in the rough and tumble cordelian market; Rodolfo Coelho Cavalcante was a master of self-promotion for 45 years and Gonçalo Ferreira da Silva in today's Rio continues the trend. This writer's knowledge of the "new" "cordel" on the internet is somewhat impressionistic, but indicates that a large percentage of internet poetry does not make it into print, or certainly most often not in the traditional format. We graciously and hopefully leave research and writing of this "cordel" to ambitious new researchers.

A significant interest in the Northeastern woodcut used to illustrate many of the covers of "cordel," sporadically since its beginnings, but significantly from the 1960s on continues today. Most interesting is that there is still a public "out there" who appreciates cordelian poetry, the traditional "romances" or "histories" as well as the circumstantial "news" story in verse. An example of the latter from the 1980s was the odyssey of Tancredo Neves and the battle for a return to democracy in Brazil after twenty-one years of military rule; Neves' tragic death in 1985 was a real "shot in the arm" for news stories.[13] In the 1990s another major event shook Brazil and was reported fully in "cordel:" the impeachment

---

13 See Curran, Mark J., "The Brazilian Democratic Dream: the View from 'Cordel'," Luzo-Brazilian Review, 2, (1986): 29-46.

of President Fernando Collor de Melo and its aftermath in the political life. Visits of Pope John Paul II to Brazil and the deaths of major national figures such as Ayrton Senna or TV actress Daniella Perez were sporadic bright moments in sales. The rise of terrorism and the wars of the Bush presidents, father and son, have garnered much interest in a plethora of new stories by contemporary poets, not to mention recent national political scandals like the "cash in the shorts"["dinheiro nas cuecas"] scandal of Brazilian political corruption.

We emphasize at this writing that it is the totality of over one hundred years of existence,[14] years of exuberance and vitality, which make "cordel" an essential part of the folk-popular cultural life of Brazil.

So what then is the value of "cordel?" If asked, the poets themselves say they express the "soul" of the people, and that they entertain, inform and instruct their readers. The writer, fan and one of the most important patrons of the poor poets from the 1950s to 1980s, Orígenes Lessa of Rio de Janeiro, said that "the poetry has value for its ingenuousness, its humor, its poetic images, its language, its classic narration and literary vitality."[15] By virtue of forty years of collecting the poetry and interaction with the poets of "cordel," this author wholeheartedly agrees and maintains that "cordel" serves a reduced and different public yet today, but for many of the same reasons as the "cordel" of the past:

It was and is in its totality one of the most successful and vibrant of folk-popular literatures in the world.

---

14 The outstanding exposition in 2001 "One Hundred Years of 'Cordel'" sponsored by SESC-POMPEIA in São Paulo and organized by curator Audálio Dantas and Joseph Luyten indelibly marked those 100 years. Local and national news coverage by major news magazines, journals, and television was significant. "Isto É", "Leitura" and even the "New York Times" reported on the event. A northeastern "fair" was recreated with representation of the principal poets at that time in Brazil; and workshops on the production of the story-poem in all phases, from writing to final printing, took place. Literally hundreds of thousands of persons came to the exhibit during the many months of the exposition, many getting to know "cordel" for the first time. It rivaled anything this writer had witnessed in previous research trips to Brazil.
15 Orígenes Lessa, "Literatura Popular em Versos," Anhembi, dezembro de 1955.

It contains much of the body of traditional, popular, narrative verse from the Portuguese (and Spanish) traditions.

It documents like no other written phenomenon the beliefs, pleasures and preoccupations of a significant part of Brazil's populace, the humble masses of the old northeast, and yet today many from the humble and middle classes representing the northeastern "Diaspora."

It entertained and continues to entertain the same public.

And finally, it teaches and informs its public of significant events of local, national and even international life.

And there is more. "Cordel" has served as a source of inspiration for the "other" culture, the learned or erudite of a sophisticated Brazil. Writers of all genres, but especially of the novel and drama, painters, makers of movies and musicians have drunk from the well spring of the humble poets who believe they were born with "the gift of verse." The list is long and impressive.

Ariano Suassuna and his colleagues from the Student Theater of Pernambuco [Teatro dos Estudantes de Pernambuco] in the 1940s and 1950s had as their goals to collect, adapt, or recreate the "popular romances of the Northeast" [o romanceiro popular nordestino] in the form of popular theater to be represented to the masses. We have as proof the now classic play "The Rogues' Trial," [Auto da Compadecida] and the trilogy "Romance of the Rock of the Kingdom," [Romance da Pedra do Reino], all written by Ariano Suassuna. Jorge Amado, still the novelist of most renown inside and outside of Brazil, was inspired by folk-popular culture and used cordelian and other popular poetry as one, among any, of his sources (see "Jubiabá," [Jubiabá], "Shepherds of the Night," [Pastores da Noite], "The Miracle Shop," [Tenda dos Milagres], and especially "Teresa Batista, Tired of War," [Tereza Batista, Cansada de Guerra].[16]

16 We worked some time ago in this area, that is, the relationship between Brazilian erudite literature and cordel. See "Influência da Literatura de Cordel na Literatura Brasileira," Revista Brasileira de Folclore (1969) 3-15; "'Grande Sertão: Veredas' e a Literatura de Cordel," Brasil-Brazil (N. 14/ ano 8/ 1995); and "Jorge Amado e a Literatura de Cordel" (Salvador da Bahia: Fundação

In theater we have the works of Alfredo Dias Gomes, "Payer of Promises," [O Pagador de Promessas], in movies the works of Glauber Rocha, in music the songs of Elba Ramalho, among others. And in addition there is the interest awakened in Brazil for the popular woodcut, [a xilogravura] which illustrates a large part of the covers of the booklets of "cordel" and attracts aficionados from the world of national and international art.[17]

So how does one describe this literature? First, let's look at the booklet of verse [o folheto] itself. It is a small booklet or pamphlet or chapbook printed on inexpensive paper, originally newsprint, with a cover of the same paper but of slightly higher quality. Recall that today's "cordel" of personal computer and printer uses a better quality paper.

Appearing at the top of the cover, normally, is the title of the story-poem which begins inside the cover on page one, for example "The Story of Charlemagne and the Twelve Knights of France," [História de Carlos Magno e os Doze Pares da França]. Below the title is the name of the author, or at times of the "author-owner" who may be the printer or small press publisher who has purchased the author's rights for that specific story-poem. More important for sales, since the very beginnings of "cordel" in the teens of the 20th century, in order to attract the attention of the potential buyer, the printer places an illustration in the center of the cover. There is a long and complex history of the cover illustrations of "cordel" (see the books already listed), but most scholars know that in its infancy, cordelian covers were quite often decorated, if they had decoration, with decorative type itself. Nevertheless, during the heyday of "cordel" from the 1920s to the end of the 1950s in the Northeast, with one large press in Recife and another later on in Juazeiro do Norte, Ceará, the pilgrimage site for Father Cícero Batista,

---

Cultural do Estado da Bahia, 1981).

17 For the popular woodcut, see the following two books: Liedo Maranhão, "The Popular Story-Poem, Its Cover and Its Illustrators [O Folheto Popular Sua Capa e Seus Ilustradores (Recife: Fundação Joaquim Nabuco – Editora Massangana, 1981) and Franklin Machado, "Cordel, Woodcuts and Illustrations," [Cordel, Xilogravuras e Ilustrações] (Rio de Janeiro: Edta., Códecri 1982). Woodcut artists like J. Borges, Abraão Batista and Marcelo Soares have exhibited and sold their works in the International Folk Market at Santa Fe, New Mexico, in recent years.

the photo-clichê dominated the covers of "cordel," using the images of movie stars, mostly from Hollywood, or images from the "romantic" postcards of Europe. But from the 1960s on the popular woodcut [a xilogravura] has been the illustration of choice judged to please the buyer in the marketplace.

The best selling booklet of "cordel" today is eight pages in length and is known most frequently as a "cordel," but during the heyday of "cordel," story-poems of 32, 48 and occasionally 60 pages were common. An anomaly was the 16 page booklet of the teens of the 20th century which often had two distinct story-poems in it. These longer poems were narrative in nature, that is, they told a story and were called "romances" [romances] or "stories," [histórias]. Because of reasons of economics (price) and popular preference, the great majority of story-poems today are eight pages in length; an exception is the production of a single large publisher in São Paulo, Editora Luzeiro Ltda. which continues to reprint cordelian classics, many 32 pages in length, with colored "comic book" style covers.[18]

Normally the poetry comes in strophes of six or seven lines of verse, called "sextilhas" or "septilhas;" with rhyme on the even verses of the sextets, abcbdb, and abcbddb on the seven line strophes. The ten line strophe [a décima] is rare and is used more in the improvised duels of the poet-singers. It is worthwhile to note that the original "cordel" often used four-line strophes [a quadra], the form most used in Portugal, but its use diminished in the beginnings of the 20th century. Another form, mnemonic in nature, was the poem of twenty-four strophes, each succeeding strophe begun by a successive letter of the Portuguese alphabet, thus the common name for it, the ABC [o ABC].

The question of authorship of the poems of "cordel" is important, especially for old "cordel" when many poets sold the rights to their verse to printers who freely claimed authorship of the same for themselves. The printers often did not bother to put the name of the true author

---

18 How Prelúdio Editora, now Luzeiro, got the rights to publish these poems is yet another story, controversial in nature. Poets like Rodoldo Coelho Cavalcante from Bahia traveled to São Paulo to protest such matters. Various studies treat the topic.

on the cover of the story-poem, even though said author received either a small quantity of money for selling his rights or more often, a fixed number of printed "folhetos" to sell in the markets. Some publishers would continue to print the poems with the name of the original author on the cover, but often put their own name on the cover followed by the term "author-owner" [autor-proprietário]. Either way, it was probably of little consolation to the real author.

The problem was complicated in 1918 with the death of "cordel's" first great author who printed his own booklets, Leandro Gomes de Barros. His widow sold at least a portion of Leandro's total works to the poet João Martins de Atayde of Recife who proceeded to reprint Leandro's poems either using the Barros name or simply putting his own name on them. Upon Atayde's death some 40 years later, his entire stock, then the greatest in all "cordel," was sold to a poet-printer in Juazeiro do Norte, Ceará, José Bernardo da Silva. The process was thus repeated, but this time the publishing shop in Juazeiro had the best of Leandro Gomes de Barros' works as well as the huge production of Atayde and the "stable" of poets he had employed in his shop in Recife, and of course, local poets in Ceará. The "Tipografia São Francisco" thus became by far the largest in "cordel" at that time.

Due to the efforts of researchers like Sebastião Nunes Batista of the Rui Barbosa Foundation in Rio de Janeiro in the 1960s and 1970s, today a large part of these important classics of early "cordel" are known by the proper names of their authors. But it is no coincidence that one of the characteristics of the booklet of "cordel" since the beginning of the 20th century is the use of the acrostic in the final strophe – a strophe or more with each succeeding line of verse beginning with the successive letters of the name of the author of the poem (notwithstanding the practice of certain printers to simply delete or change the acrostic to fit their own purposes.)

Another important characteristic of the Brazilian "cordel," at least in the 1960s and 1970s, was the colorful and lively manner in which it was displayed and sold in the marketplaces of the Northeast and later Rio de Janeiro and São Paulo. "Cordel" was sold originally in the weekly fairs of small towns in the Northeast interior and in the central markets of the large coastal cities. As the tradition evolved, poets often sold their wares at bus stations, train stations, ferry boat docks and central plazas of cities. But it was market day at the small town fair or the big city central market that were the primary places of interaction between the poet and his public. The fair or market, dating at least from the Middle Ages in Europe, was not only the distribution point of goods from small farmers, but a focal point of social life for families in the interior.[19] Its larger, permanent version, the central market in Recife, João Pessoa or Salvador, served the same purpose for most of the twentieth century in the Northeast.

The goal of the poet or oftentimes his "agent," was to attract country folks at the weekly fair or folks from the country now living in the city to listen to him "sing" or declaim his story-poem in the market, and then buy it, take it home where it would be read to others in the family, often to those who did not know how to read.[20] The procedure which really amounted to a folk-popular "performance" witnessed many times by this author was much like this:

The poet would arrive early in the morning at the marketplace, located most often in an open space of the plaza outside the "central market," and hopefully near a shade tree. He would carry his "stock" of poems in a well-used suitcase, perhaps made of cardboard or of leather. He would display the story-poems (recall the diverse types of attractive covers illustrating the poems) on a sheet of plastic or canvas on the ground, or quite often in an open suitcase resting on a stand or a sheet of wood used for the same purpose. The poems were placed quite carefully in perfect order to start the day, either in rows or like cards in a playing hand.

When sufficient people had arrived, attracted by what they knew would be both interesting and entertaining, the poet would announce

---

19 A wonderful representation of the local fair is found in Graciliano Ramos' "Barren Lives" [Vidas Secas], a classic of northeastern erudite prose.

20 This writer over the years has encountered many Brazilians from the 1960s to today, in markets and fairs, at conferences treating "cordel," or at autograph sessions for books, who told of their youth in towns in the Northeast and the custom of hearing the recitation of the verse. Many claim they learned to read and write by virtue of "cordel."

he was going to "sing" [cantar] such and such a title. If "sung," the "singing" would reflect the quality of voice of the poet. Recall it was the content of the poem, what it said, and its rhyme and rhythm that were most important. But perhaps just as often, poets would actually declaim the verses of the story-poem, for diverse reasons, perhaps because they had neither the talent or experience or voice to "sing" the poem, or perhaps because declamation was quicker. It is worthwhile to note that the "tone" of the "singing" of the poem corresponds closely to a portion of the "tones" used by the singer-poets in their poetic duels, showing the relationship that existed between the two. But regardless, the "singing" of the poem was a true performance.

The good poet knew how to use his voice, gestures, a smile, a laugh, in sum, emotions, to illustrate his story-poem. He used, like the corresponding representations of the stage, the technique of the literary aside, when he stopped "singing' or declaiming the poem and made wry comments (often in a humorous way, even using words with "double meaning") on characters or episodes in the poem. An example might be: "that cruel landholder [coronel] got what he deserved didn't he?" Occasionally but not frequently, the less timid listeners in the audience might add their own aside, or at least whisper it to the person next to them.

Upon arriving at the climactic moment of the "performance," the poet might stop the narration, saying that those who want to know the end of the story can do so by buying it right now! But there were also times when the poet did finish the entire story, depending on its length. This, then, is the process that we described first in a small book in 1973, based upon observations in the fairs and markets of the Northeast and Rio de Janeiro in 1966-1967.[21] The same performance continued through the years wherever there was the magic combination of market-poet-public; this author's observations are limited to approximately 1990. I am sure the "performance" still exists today but on a much more

---

21 Curran, A Literatura de Cordel (Recife: Imprensa Universitária, 1973).
The diary of that first wonderful year of cordelian research in Brazil exists, unpublished, but on CD with photos, by the author: "Peripécias de un Gringo Pesquisador no Brasil nos Anos 60" ["Adventures of a Gringo-Researcher in Brasil in the 1960s"].

limited scale, and perhaps modified for presentation in classrooms. But the poets themselves knew in the 1960s which colleagues "sang well," which "declaimed," and the nuances of each.

At the same time, the oral "performance" was far from the only way to sell "cordel" in that heyday of the Northeast. Oftentimes the booklets of verse were simply displayed and sold in small market-stalls, like Edson Pinto's at the Mercado São José in Recife or spread out on a piece of plastic on the street corner, or perhaps the ferry docks in Rio de Janeiro. "Cordel" was even distributed through the mail. There was one case, that of João José da Silva and his successful operation in Recife in the early 1960s, when the poet actually sent "cordel" by air freight on the old DC 3s in the Northeast!

How does one describe the "typical" cordelian author? One must distinguish between "old" "cordel," let's say, from its beginnings until approximately the mid-1960s and the poets of the recent past and a few up to the present date. The poet-singer of old "cordel" probably possessed little or no formal study, perhaps one or two years of primary school. There are anecdotes which tell of unlettered poets who asked others to write down their verse, but these were a tiny minority. Of traditional, rural roots (one of the characteristics of "old" "cordel" was its "flavor of the land or soil" with corresponding customs seen in the subject matter, themes and even language that the poets utilized), the poets were generally Catholic and conservative and probably viewed life from a folkloric point of view, that is, a world view of good and evil (that described by Luís da Câmara Cascudo in his "Five Books of the People" [Cinco Livros do Povo]. The poets were not really "political" or "politically conscious" in the current sense of the word, although they always had commented on economic, social and political issues, always from the poor man's point of view. Most of the poets were from the humble, rural class, of few monetary resources and limited economic possibilities. They were from, in the parlance of the volatile 1960s, the "dominated" class. They once again did not see the world primarily from a politically conscious point of view. They knew suffering, poverty and even misery. They could blame the rich for their woes (what folk poets have always done in world folklore), but their complaints were not expressed in terms of concrete, political, class struggle.

Only the principal poets made a living from "cordel" ("the professionals," as Rodolfo Coelho Cavalcante, leader of the poets during his times from 1955 to 1985, would say).[22] Those with most success discovered early on that if they could print as well as write their story-poems, their economic success would improve. First Leandro Gomes de Barros, and then the great entrepreneur ["empresário"] João Martins de Atayde are cases in point. The principal writers of "old" "cordel" all had in common the belief that in order to write poetry one had to have the "gift of verse," and such a gift came normally, most would say, at birth. They distinguished between the art of writing verse (the strophes, the number of syllables in a line of verse, the rhyme scheme) and the talent and inspiration of the poet. Hence, there was great pride in being able to say "I am a poet," and up to a point, they were conscious of their place in society and their special role as "poet of the people."

The cordelian poet wrote in a view common to his readers (and buyers!), an essentially moral vision with good and evil as the motivating forces behind the actions of the protagonists or characters in his story-poems. With the passage of time in the second half of the 20th century, with a new attitude garnered in part from the questions being asked them by researchers, national as well as foreign, with the efforts to "professionalize" the "career" of the cordelian poet by leaders such as Rodolfo Coelho Cavalcante between 1955 and 1985, the poet came to not only believe in his "role," but as well to propagate it in interviews and statements to the press. Thus, many poets ended up convincing themselves that they were the true "representatives of the masses," "voice of the people," and responsible, in some vague way, to the public. And such a vision was for the most part true.

Related to the concept of being "the voice of the people" is the fact that many of the principal poets of Brazilian "cordel" were and are conscious of the daunting task of pleasing their public. Many recognized correctly that if the public did not like their verse, they would not buy it. And if your poems did not sell, you would be forced

---

22 See Curran, A Presença de Rodolfo Coelho Cavalcante na Moderna Literatura de Cordel ["The Presence of Rodolfo Coelho Cavalcante in the Modern 'Literatura de Cordel'] (Rio de Janeiro: Nova Fronteira – Fundação Casa de Rui Barbosa, 1987).

to leave the "profession," [sair do ramo]. Researchers in recent years have given great importance to this matter: does the poet really represent his public or is he first, artist and thus controls his own poetic destiny?[23] The cordelian poet honest with himself never forgets his customers, the buying public, and he writes using themes, subject matter and language that he knows will please the public. He may write, on occasion, something "just for himself," and he may publish it, but this is rare, a fact confirmed in interview with the poets.

Thus one arrives at the question: what or who determines if a story-poem is good and if a poet is good? The poets themselves and their readers, through most of the 20th century, not being particularly aware of scholarly studies or capable of understanding theoretical treatises, simply and almost unanimously said that the poem is good if the public likes it. And there is no better proof than a story-poem of repeated printings. They tell tales of "folhetos" or "romances" of more than one million copies sold, a case being Leandro Gomes de Barros' famous "The Dog of the Dead" [O Cachorro dos Mortos].[24]

Another point admitted by almost all the "traditional" poets is that the good poet "knows his metrics," [não quebra a métrica]. They say you know by the end of the first page if the poet really knows how to write poetry. And the good poet always strives to improve, both in poetic expression and in style and language.

Everything said to this point about the "traditional" poet or poet of old "cordel" may not reflect many or even a majority of poets of the final decades of the 20th century. It is necessary to repeat some points previously stated of the evolution of "cordel." What is certain is that toward the end of the 20th century and beginnings of the 21st, there are significant changes. There is an entirely new generation of cordelian writers, mostly from the city or living there for many years, reflecting the rural exodus. In the 1970s, 1980s and 1990s you could find a cordelian poet more easily in the northeastern fair of Rio de Janeiro or in the Plaza of the Republic in São Paulo than in the old St. Joseph Market in Recife,

---

23 See Candace Slater's book <u>Stories on a String: the Brazilian 'Literatura de Cordel'</u>, chapter 7, the role of the poet as an original writer.
24 This number was quoted by Orígenes Lessa in <u>Anhembi</u> magazine in 1955.

the former center of Norteastern cordel! And there are many poets with significant years of formal education, many with college degrees (new Sanson Carrascos, the "graduate" in Don Quijote).

Together with place of origin or residence and level of education, there is a change in attitude by the poets, not all of them but most. The poet probably lives in an enormous city and has to deal with all the problems of the same; he probably lives extremely modestly in the economic sense, writing and printing his poems on his own while "living" from another job. He sees television daily and may be a daily visitor to the internet and is well informed of the problematic situation of living life today in the modern world, perhaps still living in Third World conditions. He probably is little idealistic and may in fact be quite cynical, expecting little from political leaders and the government of his country, although he may or may not choose to express this cynicism. The idea of expecting little from politicians was always true to some extent in "cordel," the difference being that in the old days the poets, even knowing what would happen after the elections, still held on to an almost blind optimism and hope before the election. In today's Brazil the public is less naïve or forgiving.

He may be Catholic but his Catholicism does not keep him from opening his mouth to criticize all manner of cruel reality that he and his public face today, including sacrosanct prohibitions by the "old church" prior to the second half of the 20th century. He is really disingenuous [desenganado] in the sense of being street wise and no longer naïve as to the reality that surrounds him.

The "modern" poets of Brazil applauded the end of the military dictatorship of 1964-1985 and dreamed of the "New Republic" of president-elect Tancredo Neves after the incredible popular based campaign for "direct elections" in 1984. They agonized and cried at the subsequent tragic and unjust death of the same Tancredo, this after feeling the "never before felt" national solidarity of Brazil in the days of watching and waiting before Tancredo's death. The death of a president was always an important theme in "cordel," before with Getúlio Vargas and Juscelino Kubitschek and in 1985 Tancredo Neves.

They shouted their "hurrahs" ["vivas"] and "long live Brazil" ["viva o Brasil"] before the "accidental president," José Sarney, who followed Tancredo Neves, and they waxed enthusiastic over his plan to invigorate the national economy with a new currency, the "cruzado," as well as his plan to "deputize" the public to watch for price gougers [tubarões do comércio] in supermarkets and other stores who bled the public at the beginning of Sarney's regime in 1986. Brazilians lived through a period of horrible inflation, scarcity of jobs, food and money as a result of the economic chaos of those times. They had only the hope in the future to be thankful for.

But the future has been problematic and "cordel" has reported it all -- the scandals of the handsome playboy president Fernando Collor de Mello and his impeachment in the early 1990s; the reform and economic incentives of Fernando Cardoso's regime; the victory of the man of the people – Luís Inácio da Silva or Lula by nickname – a northeasterner, migrant to São Paulo, a union man who rose through the ranks to win the presidency on his second try, and the dynamic days of economic growth in today's Brazil.

Finally, why do we dedicate ourselves to the apparently easy, but really challenging task of this book, that is, creating a bilingual anthology of Brazil's "literatura de cordel"? To answer one must explain in abbreviated form the evolution of interest in the "cordel" both within and outside of Brazil.[25] When "cordel" first attracted the attention of readers outside of its traditional buying and reading public, few people outside that public knew about "cordel" and certainly gave it little importance. The first "students" of "cordel" really were either collectors and/or Brazilian folklorists like Leonardo Mota who was much more interested in the oral and improvised verse of the poet-singer [cantador] in his books, or Gustavo Barroso who also collected early folk-popular poetry, but with more interest in the actual printed story-poems of cordel. Barroso's book "To the Sound of the Guitar" [Ao Som da Viola] is a classic commentary on "cordel." It is interesting to note that Barroso, at times, used a pseudonym on his book covers, "John of the North," [João do Norte], perhaps because he feared associating his name

---

25 At the end of the book is a bibliography of select books which tell the story in great detail.

with such a "plebian" poetry.[26] A legendary figure of Brazilian national literature, Mário de Andrade, famous poet of the Modernist Generation, appreciated "cordel" and made several trips to the Northeast and the North to record all manner of folklore but in particular to collect the story-poems of "cordel." The works collected remain at one of the best archives in Brazil at the Institute of Brazilian Studies in São Paulo. The vast works of Luís da Câmara Cascudo, formed in History by degree, an intellectual with the happy combination of sound theory as well as superb fieldwork, are among the most serious volumes ever written on both the cordelian poet and the singer-poet. Works in point are <u>Five Books of the People</u> [Cinco Livros do Povo], <u>Cowboys and Singers</u> [Vaqueiros e Cantadores] and <u>Flower of Tragic Romances</u> [Flor dos Romances Trágicos].

The interest of those already mentioned caused enthusiasm in others, including scholars from the prosperous south of Brazil. As a result, there was the first large effort on the part of a foundation and/or cultural entity in Brazil to collect and foment the study of "cordel:" the efforts of the Rui Barbosa Foundation in Rio de Janeiro under the direction of a professor of Brazilian Literature, Thiers Martins Moreira, in conjunction with a team of researchers directed by literary critic Manuel Cavalcanti Proença. The result was the systematic collection of "cordel" originals, many of the earliest texts extant, the publication of the first significant catalogue of cordelian titles, the first quality anthology and first volume of studies of the "cordel" by the then renowned researchers. Since then, significant and successive publications have included facsimile editions of rare booklets of verse, new anthologies and many monographic studies on specific topics. Aside from the aforementioned scholars, the Rui Barbosa Foundation was aided in this effort by two other respected scholars or writers -- cultural anthropologist Manuel Diégues Júnior with the principal study in the first volume of studies, and Orígenes Lessa, a true pioneer both in the collection and study of the "cordel" as well as a patron of the same.

---

26 We have known many Brazilian scholars who love "cordel" but admit privately that in the university atmosphere they cannot write about it or really be known to have an interest in it. Or, if they do dare to write on the "cordel," they must use the "theoretical" discourse of the academy.

Concurrently and as a result of such efforts, interest increased among foreign scholars: Raymond Cantel of the Sorbonne, this author from the United States, Ronald Daus of Germany, and others. Cordel became a primary topic in interviews by Raymond Cantel with the Brazilian press, including national news magazines like "Veja" ["See"] and "Manchete" ["Headline"]. Other foreigners followed, among them, Candace Slater who would do serious fieldwork and publish the best volume on the "cordel" in English (see the bibliography). The foreigners' work caught the interest of Brazilian scholars and many new researchers became active in support of "cordel." They encouraged and to some degree succeeded in establishing university level programs of study on the "cordel," including masters and Ph.D. theses and dissertations.

The new emphasis on advanced study of "cordel" brought a change in the type of studies being done; from the formerly largely descriptive and informative studies, publications evolved to the highly theoretical, employing structuralism and semiotics. One innovation, still in the 1970s and early 1980s were studies sponsored by research institutions both on the state and national level, but now utilizing informants from "cordel" or even the principal poets of "cordel" of the times, that is, the poets and publishers themselves. José Alves Sobrinho, Franklin Machado, Rodolfo Coelho Cavalcante and others present the perspective of the artist himself.

Along with the studies, and really a correlative of them, were the many anthologies of "cordel" over the years (see the bibliography which follows). There were several good ones, from the original by the Rui Barbosa Foundation in 1962 to the effort by Sebastião Nunes Batista, sponsored by a bank in the Northeast. One successful anthology by a publishing house in São Paulo in the 1970s sold some 20,000 copies, a huge response for the modest "cordel." Since those early efforts there has been a small "explosion" of works on cordel. This author was requested to do a bilingual anthology of the "cordel" for publication in Spain, a work published in 1991; and this current bilingual anthology in English is an offshoot of that published in Madrid. Hedra Publishing Company has recently done a series of anthologies of individual cordelian poets with introductions by scholars in the field.

So we arrive at the end of this introduction of the "cordel" to the reader and the purpose of the current book. First of all, we know of no serious English-Portuguese anthology of the "cordel," and the topic deserves the attention of the wider audience of speakers of English who do not know Portuguese. Because this modest volume does not have as its purpose the study or analysis of "cordel," but rather the presentation of the poetry itself to a new reading audience, it does not enter into discussion of theoretical questions or critical models. Our purpose is to present within a limit of relatively few pages (in comparison to the very large monolingual anthologies of "cordel" in Brazil) a good sampling of the phenomenon.

We are limited by the sheer size of "cordel," a body of story-poems numbering perhaps up to one hundred thousand titles, an estimate of Joseph Luyten, Brazilian researcher of the "cordel," but base our selection first and foremost on our own collection compiled over forty years in Brazil. And in part, we see this modest anthology as a small companion book to the much larger "Portrait of Brazil in the 'Cordel,'" [Retrato do Brasil em cordel], an encyclopedic overview of the story-poems available on CD from the author and soon available in Portuguese at the Ateliê Press of São Paulo.

We are including the maximum number of story-poems of the standard eight pages in length but adding one sample of the poetic duel and one example of the long, narrative story-poem ["romance" or "história,"] simply from the point of view of practicality. Since it is impossible to present all or even a majority of the themes of cordel, we choose ten titles representative of the whole, keeping in mind the ten chapters of "Portrait," a Brazilian poetic odyssey. The titles are, in addition, representative of the whole of "cordel" and are from the earliest times up to the near present.

We include a short introduction before each story-poem which speaks of the author (when known) and the subject matter or topic of the booklet in verse. The objective is to place the poem in context within the totality of "cordel" and the Brazilian reality it describes. In the story-poems themselves, we respect the original text of the poet which reflects his idiosyncrasies of spelling, punctuation and syntax.

We do not correct grammatical errors of expression like agreement between subject and verb or pronoun and verb which at times reflect regional or particular use of the poet. There are occasions, and they are not few, when we have retained the original Portuguese word in the English translation, the reason being to maintain the flavor and tone of the Portuguese original. In such cases we utilize footnotes to either translate or explain the term. All our efforts will be worthwhile if the reader enjoys the marvelous world of "cordel" written by these gifted poets who sincerely believe that they are the "voice of the masses" of northeastern Brazil.

THE STORY - POEMS OF "CORDEL"

Leandro Gomes de Barros, perhaps "cordel's" most famous author.

1

"Debate of the Protestant Preacher with Master Vulture"
"Debate d'um Ministro Nova-Seita e Urubú"
Attributed to Leando Gomes de Barros

This story-poem by the master Leandro Gomes de Barros is an excellent example of northeastern popular poetic expression, and this in itself would give him a predominant place in this anthology. But there is another reason for the presence of this poem: in this writer's opinion it may best express the conservative, "old church" and folkloric view of religion, perhaps the largest of themes in the "literatura de cordel." Thus it is fitting that this cordelian poem by perhaps its best pioneer author opens this anthology.

"Cordel" truly documents the entire folk-popular religious odyssey of the northeasterner: the traditional story-poems of the life and sufferings of Jesus, those dedicated to the life of the Virgin Mary, St. Peter and other principal Catholic saints, those of the numerically large theme of the devil and all his mischievousness, the stories treating the Brazilian "messianic" figures and the resulting popular cults dedicated to them: especially to Father Cícero Romão Batista of Juazeiro do Norte, Ceará and Friar Damian, the long-lived Franciscan missionary famous for the annual missions in the backlands. And finally, "cordel" treats the famous Brazilian syncretism of religion in its story-poems which mix the elements of Catholic with indigenous and Afro-Brazilian spiritualism.

One aspect among many of the vast religious universe seen in "cordel" must be the portrait of an important phenomenon in the age of Leandro Gomes de Barros at the beginnings of the 20th century. The presence of the first Protestant missionaries in this the most Catholic and traditional region of Brazil presented a real challenge to the old ways. The relative isolation of the region had caused the Northeast to become the cradle of amazing figures like "Anthony the Counselor" [Antônio Conselheiro] in the novel "The War at the End of the World" [A Guerra do Fim do Mundo] by Mário Vargas Llosa, renowned Peruvian novelist, a novel inspired by "Rebellion in the Backlands" [Os Sertões] by Euclides da Cunha. Even more important would be the case of Father Cícero Romão Batista, an icon of the Northeast.

One of the main protagonists of "Debate …" is the "New Sect" [Nova Seita] Protestant Preacher, the name given to the early Protestant ministers and their flocks in late 19th century northeast by the humble natives of the area. There in fact was an atmosphere of suspicion, ignorance and even aversion when the first missionaries arrived in the Northeast at the end of the 19th century, something perfectly documented in this poem.

Along with the famous debates between traditional Catholics and Protestants, there were other story-poems treating local customs; the well-known discussions [discussões] in regard to moral issues, notably the use of alcohol in its primary northeastern form, sugar cane rum [cachaça]. The same Leandro Gomes de Barros penned at least a dozen cordelian poems praising the local firewater, including his "Hail Mary of Sugar Cane Rum," and he was known to enjoy a libation before a session of improvising verse for friends and customers.[27]

Leandro Gomes de Barros captures in this poem the debate about customs and the essence of the "Old Church" of the northeastern interior: fasting during Lent, Midnight Mass, the annual Holy Mission and especially the role of the **Bible** and the debate of the role of the Virgin Mary between old school Catholics and some Protestant groups. The fact Leandro chose an ugly, black vulture to be the paladin of the faith (the common vulture was often portrayed as the "garbage collector of the Northeast") was a touch of irony in this the most ironic of all the poets of "cordel." The vulture in effect becomes another variation of the northeastern version of the anti-hero; in this case the poor, ugly, mistreated and miserable rogue who lives and survives through his intelligence and "street smarts" in a cruel, unforgiving world. Famous

---

27 See our book <u>A Literatura de Cordel</u> (Recife: University of Pernambuco Press, 1973).

protagonists in "cordel" like John Cricket [João Grilo], Pedro Quengo and Pedro de Malasartes are all sons of the picaresque tradition of the Iberian Peninsula and northeastern adaptations of the same.

"Debate between a Protestant Preacher and Master Vulture"	"Debate d'um Ministro Nova-Seita com Urubú"
Attributed to Leandro Gomes de Barros	Atribuído a L. G. de Barros

I'm going to tell you a story	Vou contar-vos uma história
That took place a little while back:	Que há pouco tempo se deu:
An old Protestant lady	Uma velha nova-seita
Went out to get wood and died.	Foi buscar lenha e morreu.
A vulture came upon her	Um urubu achou ela
And said, "Here's where I get mine."	E disse: aqui tiro o meu!
The preacher when he found out,	O Ministro, quando soube,
Exclaimed, "This is the devil's business!"	Exclamou, "Isto é do Droga!"
If naked sister died,	Se a irmã pelada morreu,
The devil's got him a mother-in-law,	Ganha o diabo uma sogra,
We lose her from the cult	Nós a perdemos do culto
And the devil is the one who gets her.	E o diabo é quem a logra!
Master Vulture saw the old lady	Mestre Urubu viu a véia
Where she kicked the bucket.	Onde esticou a canela.
He said to the other vultures:	Disse aos outros urubus:
Hey good buddies, let's go get her!	Meus maninhos, vamos a ela!
Until God sends something different	Enquanto Deus não manda outra
Let's just chew on that one!	Vamos roendo naquela!
Then the preacher showed up,	O Ministro aí chegou,
Saying, this old one is mine.	Dizendo: Esta velha é minha.
She was one of the Protestants	Era uma da nova-seita
Who had joined our flock.	Que no nosso culto vinha.
The vulture retorted: I swear!	O Urubu respondeu: Votes!
Take that old devil then.	Carregue, então sua tinha.
"Devil no," said the Preacher,	--Tinha não! disse o Ministro,
She was a devout lady.	Ela era nossa devota.
Master Vulture asked:	Perguntou Mestre Urubu:
Where did this disaster come from,	De onde veio esta derrota,
Stinking up our countryside	Empestar o nosso campo
With this horrible ground hog smell?	Com esta horrível marmota?

The Preacher said: Vulture	Disse o Ministro: Urubu
It's proven you have no soul;	Não tens alma, está provado;
But you ought to get religion	Porém devias ter crença
And not be so obstinate.	E não ser tão obstinado.
Do you want to become a Protestant?	Queres ser da nova-seita?
Then you can be baptized.	Lá, tu serás batisado.
Said then Master Vulture:	Disse então, Mestre Urubu:
You've got it all wrong,	Você vai mal de receita,
I've got it in my heart to love you,	Coração tenho p'ra amar-te,
But you're in with the Protestants,	Mas estás na nova-seita,
And you are one of the ones, when they die,	E és um dos que, quando morrem,
Not even the hide's any good!	Nem o couro se aproveita!
The Preacher responded:	O Ministro respondeu:
My soul is valued	Minha alma é aproveitada
By the angels of the Lord	Pelos anjos do Senhor
And will be taken up to heaven.	Há de ser ao céu levada.
The vulture answered him:	O Urubu lhe respondeu:
That's crazy; no way!	Isto é loucura, vai nada!
Don't you find more poetry	Não achas mais poesia
In the old religion?	Na velha religião?
Fasting during Lent,	Jejuar pela Quaresma,
Setting off fireworks on St. John's Day,	Soltar fogos em São João,
Going to mass on Christmas Eve,	Ir a missa do Natal
Attending the Holy Mission?[28]	Ouvir a Santa Missão?
-- That no! said the preacher.	-- Isso não! Disse o Ministro.
I just have to follow Jesus,	Eu hei de seguir Jesus,
Because it was He who saved me.	Porque foi quem me salvou.
He is my guide and my light.	É meu guia e minha luz.
Then the vulture asked him:	Perguntou-lhe o Urubu:
How come you're mad at the cross?	Porque tem raiva da cruz?

---

28 The annual Mission is an old Catholic custom. The mission was a mechanism to bring the teachings of the faith and the sacraments to a distant or isolated place or region that did not have a regular priest, parish or Catholic school. Father Damian of cordelian fame was one of the most famous preachers of missions in Brazil, working in the backlands for over fifty years. In the early days of Portugese colonization, the Jesuit Order was known for such endeavors, although Damian was a Franciscan.

Was it not on it that died	Não foi nela que morreu
Our Lord Jesus Christ?	Nosso Senhor Jesus Cristo?
The blood that He shed	O sangue que derramou
Have you not seen on the cross?	Você na cruz não tem visto?
You know, you just bring abuse.	De você só vem abuso.
We're not getting anywhere here.	Convém acabar com isto!
And why did that dead protestant	E por que essa nova-seita
Detest Our Lady,	Detesta a Nossa Senhora,
Being clearer than the day	Sendo mais clara que o dia
More pure than the dawn?	Sendo mais pura que a aurora?
The protestant when he dies	O nova-seita, morrendo,
Won't see heaven, not even from the outside.	Não vê o céu, nem por fora.
What's the advantage in believing in Christ	Que vantagem crer em Cristo
And not believing in the Virgin Mary?	Sem crer na Virgem Maria?
Didn't Jesus have a mother	Jesus não teve uma mãe
Like the scripture says?	Como diz a profecia?
How can you deny that,	Como vocês negam isto,
You bunch of hypocrites?	Usando de hipocrisia?
I may be a vulture, but I believe	Eu sou urubu, mas creio
And I swear by my faith it's the truth,	Juro por fé na verdade,
That Mary was born pure,	Que Maria nasceu pura,
And is part of the Divinity.	Faz parte da Divindade.
She gave birth to Jesus Christ	Deu a luz a Jesus Cristo
And still remained a virgin!	Conservando a virgindade!
Then said the Protestant:	Então disse o nova-seita:
Vulture, you are mistaken,	Urubu, estás enganado,
I've studied the whole Bible	Eu estudei toda a Bíblia,
And I'm grounded in it.	Estou nela baseado.
Master Vulture asked:	Mestre Urubu perguntou:
So you say? You're way behind me.	Quem? Você me anda atrasado.
The protestant said: No!	Disse o nova-seita: Não!
I am saved by Jesus.	Estou salvo por Jesus.
The vulture answered him:	O Urubu lhe respondeu:
Easier for water to give light,	Mais fácil água dar luz,
The sun turn into ice,	O sol ficar como gelo,
The devil carry the cross!	O demo andar com a cruz!

I who fly way high up there,
I've got other inspiration.
I fly very near to heaven,
And I never presumed your idea,
And besides, when you die,
You'll end up right under the ground.

Now, I and the eagles
Santos Dumont, Ferramenta[29]
We fly way up high,
In the place where there is no wind
And on one of those trips,
One day one of us will get in [into heaven].

The protestant answered:
I'm counting on victory.
When I die, I'm going to heaven,
I'll end up living in glory.
The vulture answered him:
Your story is going no where!

Then the protestant said:
I believe in my Savior.
For it was He who died for me,
He was my Redeemer.
The vulture asked him:
-- Didn't Our Lord have a mother?

Didn't Mary remain a virgin,
After giving birth to Our Lord?
Was it not the Holy Spirit
Who enabled her to conceive?
And why do the Protestants
Believe in one and not the other?

Eu, que vou até lá em cima,
Tenho uma outra inspiração.
Vou até perto do céu,
Nunca tive esta intenção,
Quanto mais, você que morre,
E vai p'ra baixo do chão.

Pois agora, eu com as águias
Santos Dumont, Ferramenta,
Vamos até muito em cima,
No lugar onde não venta
E, numa viagem dessas,
Lá um dia um de nós entra!

Respondeu o nova-seita:
Eu conto com a vitória.
Quando morrer, vou ao céu,
Fico morando na Glória.
O Urubu lhe respondeu:
Vai bem mal sua história!

Então, disse o nova-seita:
Creio no meu Salvador.
Pois foi quem morreu por mim,
Foi Ele o meu Redentor.
O Urubu lhe perguntou:
-- Não teve mãe o Senhor?

Maria não ficou virgem,
Depois do Senhor nascer?
Não foi o Espírito Santo
Que fez ela conceber?
E por que a nova-seita
Crê num e noutro não crer?

---

29 Santos Dumont is the Brazilian who in 1901 flew a dirigible above the Eiffel Tower in Paris and later in 1906 flew a heavier-than-air-machine. In Brazil he is considered the Father of Aviation, prior to the Wright brothers. Ferramenta is the nickname of the Portuguese pilot, Antônio da Costa Bernardes, born on July 25, 1870, in Vila Nova de Gaia, Portugal, deceased on July 25, 1907, in the same place where he built his airplane "O Português" and made his first flight on April 2, 1904. Later on he carried out other dirigible flights in Portugal and Brazil.

Those hymns of yours	Esses hinos de vocês
What do they have to do with religion?	Que influem na religião?
A good Brazilian samba	Mais vale um samba de palmas
Is worth more than your devotion.	Do que a sua devoção.
Even a vulture like me	Um urubu como eu sou
Prays better than that.	Faz melhor sua oração.
Well, said the protestant:	Então, disse o nova-seita:
I've studied the Bible,	A Bíblia tenho estudado,
I've seen what God wrote,	Vi o que Deus escreveu,
I'm faithful to his commands.	Sou fiel ao seu mandado.
The vulture answered him:	O Urubu lhe respondeu:
You were excommunicated!	Você foi excomungado!
I don't even want to see you any more,	Eu nem quero ve-lo mais,
You come around here just to bedevil me,	Você vem me inquizilar,
A goblin of a Protestant	Caipora de nova-seita
Is dangerous even to the touch.	É danada p'ra pegar,
Take that devil of an old woman,	Leve o diabo da velha,
Or eat her or bury her!	Ou coma, ou mande enterrar!
Master Vulture stretched his wings	Mestre Urubu bateu asas
And said: C'mon gang let's get out of here!	E disse: Vamos negrada!
Let's not chew on this old lady,	Não comamos desta velha,
She's damnation personified!	Que ela está amaldiçoada!
A vulture could lose his beak	Um urubu perde o bico,
Gnawing on this heretic!	Se come esta excomungada!
Wait, said the Protestant:	Então, disse o nova-seita:
My sister is no devil!	Minha irmã não é quisila!
The vulture said: -- Well, this one	Disse o Urubu: -- Pois esta
Could disgrace an entire town.	Faz desgraçar uma vila.
Because of her the devil	Por causa dela, o diabo
Lost the whole thing.	Perdeu até a mochila.

Well, said the Protestant:	Então, disse o nova-seita:
May the devil pursue you!	Que o diabo te persiga!
And the vulture said: and I to you,	E o Urubu disse: Eu a tí,
Protestant – you get the curse![30]	Nova-Seita, dou-te figa!
You, wherever you go, leave a trail	Tú, onde vais, deixas o rasto
Of hunger, pestilence and intrigue.	Da fome, pestes e intriga!
I, being a mere pagan brute	Eu, sendo um bruto pagão
I believe in and follow the Commandments	Creio e sigo os mandamentos.
And you, being baptized,	E tu, sendo batizado,
You deny the teachings,	Negas os ensinamentos,
And you run like a condemned dog,	Corres, como um cão danado,
If we talk about sacraments!	Se se fala em sacramentos!
A saint who happened to be near by,	Um santo que estava ali perto,
And the devil as well,	Como o diabo, também,
-- Bravo! was what he said,	-- Bravos! era o que dizia,
This vulture says it well!	Este Urubu fala bem!
May this vile protestant die!	Morra este vil protestante!
And the devil said, "Amen!"	E o diabo disse: Amem!
End	Fim

---

[30] A liberal translation for a very Brazilian gesture: making the hand into a fist and inserting the thumb between first and second finger (forming a rough cross). It has many connotations: "God help me" from you; "you devil, away with you;" "to hell with you;" and even "up yours"! The Italians have a similar and larger gesture, bending the right arm at the elbow and slapping the right bicep with the left palm. The Brazilians, along the same line, use the same gesture, saying "A banana for you!" ["Uma banana pr'a você."] The reader gets the idea.

Cover of the story-poem "Money"
by Leandro Gomes de Barros

2.

"Money"
"O Dinheiro"
Leandro Gomes de Barros

    This second poem in our anthology was penned by the one and same "cordel" virtuoso Leandro Gomes de Barros, author of "The Debate of the Protestant Minister with Master Vulture." No one was more present to the backlands farmer, the small town merchant or even a coastal city dweller than the protagonists of this story-poem: the ubiquitous parish priest or his boss the bishop who actually ordained the priests from the seminaries and came to the local parishes to confirm youngsters in the faith. "Money" is really a morality story, a poetic-philosophic statement on the power and evils of money in the world. Perhaps it is only a coincidence that a simple vicar and not so simple bishop cannot resist its seductions, even in the old Northeast.

    But there are other reasons for choosing "Money." First of all this is a fine poem, well written in the sense of language, rhyme and meter in the unbeatable satiric style of Leandro Gomes de Barros – other poets might come close to matching his ideas or satire, but very few combined the style and thought of the old master. Secondly, the poem became one of the three basic texts "borrowed" and recreated by the icon of Northeastern literature, playwright Ariano Suassuna in his "The Rogues' Trial" ["Auto da Compadecida"]. And finally, but not the least, the catalyst for action in the little drama is a figure familiar to Brazil at the time of Leandro Gomes de Barros and representative of economic development and international capitalism at the time – the Englishman. It was England with its capitalists and engineers who developed the railway system in Brazil in the early twentieth century. Leandro penned several other satires of them, but "Dinheiro" is the best.

Mark J. Curran

"Money"	"O Dinheiro"
Leandro Gomes de Barros	Leandro Gomes de Barros
Recife, 1909	Recife, 1909

Money in this world,[31]
There's no way to defeat it,
Nor danger that can confront it,
Nor social rank that commands it.
Everything is below it.
Only it is the all powerful.

O dinheiro neste mundo,
Não há força que o debande,
Nem perigo que o enfrente,
Nem senhoria que mande.
Tudo está abaixo delle.
Só elle alli é o grande.

[Money] rules over a throne
Surrounded by ambition,
Flattery at its feet,
Always at its disposition,
Asking it with care:
-- Is there anything I can do for you, Master?

Elle impera sobre um throno
Cercado por ambição,
O chaleirismo a seus pés,
Sempre está de promptidão,
Perguntando-lhe com cuidado:
-- O que lhe falta, patrão?

In money has been seen
Unrecognized nobility,
Means that win court cases
Even when these are lost causes,
Honor through infamy
Glory badly acquired.

No dinheiro tem se visto
Nobreza desconhecida,
Meios que ganham questão
Ainda estando perdida,
Honra por meio da infamia
Gloria mal adquerida.

Because money only
Has a greater use,
It is the light that shines most brilliantly
In the realm of society.
The code of that time is it [money]
With the law according to its will.

Porque só mesmo o dinheiro
Tem maior utilidade,
É o pharol que mais brilha
Perante a sociedade.
O codigo dalli é elle
A lei é sua vontade.

---

31 Because of the date of composition and printing, 1909, early in Leandro's career, the spelling of the Portuguese is of that time, before several modifications and modernizations in the twentieth century. We choose to maintain the original Portuguese of the facsimile edition of the prestigious and careful Rui Barbosa Foundation edition of the poem in: "O Dinheiro. Casamento do Sapo. Últimas Palavras dum Papa" IN: <u>Antologia Tomo V. Leandro Gomes de Barros</u> Rio de Janeiro: Ministério da Educação e Cultura, Fundação Casa de Rui Barbosa - Universidade Federal da Paraíba, 1980. Because it is a facsimile edition of the original rare text, the punctuation is that of the original and does not follow today's norms.

A man having money	O homem tendo dinheiro
Kills his own father.	Mata o próprio pae.
Justice closes its eyes,	A justiça fecha os olhos,
The police don't show up there,	A polícia lá não vai,
Five or six months go by	Passam-se cinco ou seis mezes
Time goes by, the case disappears.	Vai indo, o processo cae.
[The defendant] buys five witnesses	Compra cinco testemunhas
Who testify in his favor,	Que depõe a seu favor,
He rents two scribes	Aluga dois escrivães
And buys off the prosecuting attorney.	E compra o procurador.
He plies two lawyers with silver,	Faz dois doutores de prata,
Ready to serve, my lord.	Prompto o homem, meu senhor.
And even if the case goes to the jury	Ainda que vá a jury
He then buys a delay,	Compra logo a attenuante,
Greases the palms of the jury	Dá um uncto nos jurados
And is freed at that instant.	Se livra no mesmo instante,
The judge rules in his favor,	Tem o juiz a favor,
Jury, so on and so forth.	Jurados e assim por deante.
These very serious cases	Essas questões muito serias
Which go before the tribunal,	Que vão para o tribunal,
Where certain papers are necessary	Alli exige papéis
Which carry legal proof,	Que levem prova legal,
Bank notes of 500 in value	Cedulas de quinhentos fachos,
Provide the principal paper.	É o papel principal.
Money creates eloquence	Dinheiro faz eloquencia
In someone who never studied,[32]	A quem nunca teve estudo,
Imprints courage on the weak,	Imprime coragem ao fraco,
And animates everyone.	Dá animação a tudo.
Wins battles without arms,	Vence batalha sem arma,
Playing the role of lance and shield.	Faz vez de lança e escudo.
Where there is no money,	Aonde não há dinheiro
Every effort is lost,	Todo trabalho é perdido,
Every case fades,	Toda questão esmorece,
Every business dealing fails,	Todo negocio é fallido,
Every calculation turns out in error,	Todo calculo é errado,
Every debate is defeated.	Todo debate é vencido.

---

32 The line refers to another topic dear to the poet: those who buy university degrees, seen in the poem "The Doctors of '60 [Os Doutores de 60].

Mark J. Curran

So it is that a man with no money	Pois um homem sem dinheiro
Is like a demented old man,	É como um velho demente,
A cat without claws,	Um gato que não tem unha,
A serpent without fangs,	Cobra que não tem um dente,
A dog with no sense of smell,	Cachorro que não tem faro,
A horse, thin and sickly.	Cavallo magro e doente.
Because in facing money	Porque perante o dinheiro
Everything becomes soft,	Tudo alli se torna molle,
Because there is no object	Porque não há objecto
That does not roll under its feet.	Que sobre seus pés não role.
Give money to a dead man	Bote o dinheiro no morto
And watch his bones start moving.	Que a ossada delle bole.
The university graduate after money	O bacharel por dinheiro
Is like a monkey after a banana	Só macaco por banana
Or a cat after a rat	Ou gato por guabirú[33]
Or a racoon[34] after sugar cane	Ou um guaxinim por canna
Or a small monkey after its juice	Só saguim[35] pela rizina
Or a goat after green plants.	Ou bode por gitirana.[36]
A young maiden having money	A moça tendo dinheiro
Being as ugly as death,	Sendo feia como a morte,
Paints herself up, dresses up,	Caracterisa-se, enfeita-se,
And always betters her luck.	Sempre melhora de sorte.
More than a thousand adventurers	Mais de mil aventureiros
Desire her as a consort.	A desejam por consorte.
Since money on this earth	Porque dinheiro na terra
Is a cape that covers everything.	É capa que tudo encobre.
Cover a dog with gold	Cubra um cachorro com ouro
And it turns into nobility.	Que elle tem que ficar nobre.
He's superior to his owner	É superior ao dono
Perhaps when the owner is poor.	Se acaso o dono fôr pobre.

---

33 The "guabirú" is a common rat in the Northeast.
34 "Racoon" is the closest we can come to the "guaxinim" or "mão pelada," a raccoon-like animal of the region.
35 The "saguim" is a small monkey with a long tail.
36 "Gitirana" or "jiritana" is a climbing plant of the region which produces many flowers in season.

I came upon a story told	Eu vi narrar um facto
That astonished me.	Que fiquei admirado.
A backlander told me	Um sertanejo me disse
That during this last century	Que nesse seculo passado
He witnessed a funeral for a dog	Viu enterrar um cachorro
With honors of a potentate.	Com honras de um potentado.
An Englishman had a dog	Um inglêz tinha um cachorro
One of great esteem.	De uma grande estimação.
Said dog kicked the bucket	Morreu o dito cachorro
And the Englishman said, "So …	E o inglêz disse então:
… Me buries that dog	Mim enterra esse cachorro
Even if I have to spend a million."[37]	Inda que gaste um milhão.
He went to the vicar and said to him:	Foi ao vigario lhe disse:
My dog died	Morreu cachorra de mim
And the vultures[38] in Brazil	E urubú no Brasil
Can't be allowed to do him in.	Não poderá dar-lhe fim,
-- Did said dog leave any money,	-- Cachorro deixou dinheiro,
The vicar asked then?	Perguntou o vigário, assim?
-- Me want to bury dog.	-- Mim quer enterrar cachorro
The vicar said: oh, Englishman!	Disse o vigário: oh! inglêz!
Do you think that this	Você pensa que isto aqui
Is your country?[39]	É o paíz de vocês?
The Englishman said: oh! doggy!	Disse o inglez: oh! cachorro!
We'll have to spend everything this time.	Gasta tudo esta vez.

---

37 Throughout the entire scenes when the Englishman speaks, the poet Leandro portrays him using a fractured Portuguese with all types of common errors – incorrect subject pronouns with respective verbs, lack of pronouns when necessary, and so forth.

38 Once again the ever present vultures of Brazil are mentioned in a Leandro Gomes de Barros poem, but this time in their usual role as the "garbage men" of north Brazil, that is, eaters of carrion.

39 As we mentioned in the introduction, the role of English capital and know-how was ever present in the late 19th and early twentieth centuries in Brazil, including the Northeast, in the construction of the railways. The Englishman with his arrogance, white linen suit, and still present memories of Empire was satirized by the poet throughout his career from the late 19th century until his death in 1918.

The dog, before expiring,	Elle antes de morrer
Readied a last will and testament	Um testamento apromptou
Just four thousand [40]	Só quatro contos de réis
He left for you the vicar.	Para o vigario deixou.
Before the Englishman could finish	Antes do inglez findar
The vicar let out a huge sigh.	O vigario suspirou.
-- Poor thing,! said the vicar.	-- Coitado!, disse o vigario.
What did the unfortunate thing die from?	De que morreu esse pobre?
What an intelligent animal!	Que animal intelligente!
Such a noble sentiment!	Que sentimento tão nobre!
Before departing this world	Antes de partir do mundo
He made me a present of the "dough."	Fez-me presente do cobre.
Take him to the cemetery	Leve-o para o cemiterio
And I'll be right there for the burial	Que vou o encommendar
That is, be sure and bring the money	Isto é, traga o dinheiro
Before he is actually buried,	Antes delle se enterrar,
"Pay me later" arrangements	Estes suffragios fiados
May risk his salvation.	É fativo não salvar.
And so the dog arrived there	E lá chegou o cachorro
And with the money right in front of him,	O dinheiro foi na frente,
The funeral had its prayers,[41]	Teve memento o enterro,
Full fledged funeral mass with body present,	Missa de corpo presente,
Litany and all that goes with it	Ladínha e seu rancho
Better than for many human beings.	Melhor do que certa gente.
Somebody sent word to the bishop	Mandaram dar parte ao bispo
Telling what the vicar had done	Que o vigario tinha feito
The burial of a dog	O enterro do cachorro.
Was something that just wasn't right.	Que não era de direito.
The bishop at that point had a lot to say	O bispo ahi fallou muito
Showing him to be quite out of sorts.	Mostrou-se mal satisfeito.

---

40 In the early twentieth century, a "conto" was at least the equivilant of "a thousand" in today's money; four "contos" would be a significant amount of money, reckoning $4000 dollars.

41 Said prayers, "memento" in Portuguese, are part of the prayers of the canon of the mass for the dead, specifically said for the soul of the deceased..

He ordered the vicar to come see him	Mandou chamar o vigário
And the vicar arrived very shortly thereafter	Prompto o vigário chegou
At your service, Your Excellency …	As ordens sua excellencia …
The bishop asked him:	O bispo lhe perguntou:
So what dog was this	Então que cachorro foi
That you Mr. Vicar just buried?	Que seu vigario enterrou?
It was an important dog	Foi um cachorro importante
An animal of intelligence	Animal de intelligencia
He before dying	Elle antes de morrer
Left Your Excellency	Deixou a vossa excellencia
Two thousand in gold	Dois contos de reis em ouro …
If I made a mistake, please have patience.	Se errei, tenha paciencia.
It wasn't an error, no, Mr. Vicar,	Não foi erro, sr. vigario,
You are a good pastor	Você é um bom pastor
Please pardon me for inconveniencing you	Desculpe eu incommodál-o
The fault is with the carrier of the message,	A culpa é do portador,
A dog like this one	Um cachorro como este
One can see that he is deserving.	Já vê que é merecedor.
An informant of mine told me	O meu informante disse-me
That the case had taken place	Que o caso tinha se dado
Therefore I judged that that it must have involved	E eu julguei que isso fosse
A wretch of a dog.	Um cachorro desgraçado.
The dog remembered me	Elle lembrou-se de mim
I'm not one to scorn him for that.	Não o faço desprezado.
Then the vicar opened up	O vigário ahi abriu
The package of two thousand	Os dois contículos de reis.
The bishop said: that's better	O bispo disse: é melhor
Than many of the faithful do.	De que diversos fieis.
And he said: May God provide	E disse: prouvera Deus
Ten more to die the same way.	Que assim lá morresse uns dez.
So if it were not for money,	E se não fosse o dinheiro
The case would have turned ugly,	A questão ficava feia,
The dog would have been dug up	Desenterrava o cachorro
The vicar would have gone to jail.	O vigario ia a cadeia.
But since the "scratch" was flowing	Mas como gimbre correu
It all ended like writing in the sand.	Ficou qual lettras na areia.

Mark J. Curran

Judas was a holy man	Judas era um homem santo
He was preaching the religion	Pregava a religião
He was a disciple of Christ	Era discípulo de Christo
And thus had every means of learning	Tinha toda direcção
But for thirty coins	Porém por 30 dinheiros
He dispensed with his own salvation.	Dispensou a salvação.
Money alone cannot	O dinheiro só não pode
Keep its owner from dying,	Privar do dono morrer,
Stop the wind in the air	Parar o vento no ar
And deter the rain.	E prohibir de chuver.
Everything else becomes easy	O resto torna-se facil
For money to make money.	Para o dinheiro dinheiro fazer.
The priest [is] in the temple	O sacerdote no templo
In the midst of his sermon.	Ainda estando no sermão.
An atheist enters the church	Chega um atheu na egreja
Bringing him one half million.	E traga-lhe um meio milhão.
He goes right up to the priest	Que elle vae logo encontral-o
And slaps it right into the palm of his hand.	Bota-o na palma da mão.
Having a lot of money,	Havendo muito dinheiro,
A sister can marry a brother.	Casa-se irmã com irmão.
The bishop takes one forth of it,	O bispo dispensa um quarto,
Another fifth goes to the Pope.	Vai ao papa outro quinhão.
The vicar greases the palms	O vigário dar-lhe o uncto
So why shouldn't they get married?	E porque não casam então?
Fim	Fim

Cover of the story-poem "The Girl Who Beat Up Her Mother and Was Turned into a Dog" by Rodolfo Coelho Cavalcante

3.

"The Girl Who Beat Up Her Mother and Was Turned into a Dog"
"A Moça que Bateu na Mãe e Virou Cachorra"
Rodolfo Coelho Cavalcante

This story-poem is from the cordelian classic genre of the "example," a didactic narrative poem that presents a moral lesson. Included in the Brazilian northeastern variant are "examples interpreted as punishment inflicted upon mankind by a divinity, that is, the nation punished and the people disobeying the powers of the Messiah."[42] The "examples" have their origin in the religious and moral traditions of the late Middle Ages in diverse countries of Christian Europe when writers both religious and secular treated social customs and the vices and virtues of man. The means used were of the most diverse: sermons from the pulpit employing stories, fables and legends (some of Middle Eastern origin) and books of stories with themes similar to those in the sermons. One case in point of the story with a moral lesson at its end was Spain's <u>Count Lucanor</u> [El Conde Lucanor] by Don Juan Manuel (1282-1348). The basic source in Portuguese, coming a bit later, was <u>Stories and Story Poems of Profit and Example</u> [Contos e Histórias de Proveito e Exemplo] by Gonçalo Fernandes Trancoso (c. 1585). The word "example" [exemplo] is used yet today in many variations of the old "example" tradition, but now throughout Latin America.

The evolved form of this old tradition which is found today in Brazil's cordelian poetry is a dynamic and lively form which employs the following structure: the sinner is converted into a monster or animal for mistreating family members or for being unfaithful to the faith tradition of traditional Roman Catholicism, or yet of making fun of religion or persons associated with religion. Then the sinner has to wander the earth, suffering, and doing evil as opposed to living happily on the road to God. All this takes place in a story-poem of eight pages in length in sextets or septets with <u>xaxaxa</u> or <u>ababccb</u> rhyme.

---

42 This quotation translated to English is from a book by Liedo Maranhão, <u>Classificação Popular da Literatura de Cordel</u> (Petrópolis: Editora Vozes, 1976).

The well-known cordelian poet Rodolfo Coelho Cavalcante was a master of the poetic "example." More than fifty per cent of his total cordelian production is based on this form.[43] Calvalcante claimed authorship to more than one thousand, seven hundred individual cordelian titles in a career lasting almost fifty years from the beginning of the 1940s to his tragic, accidental death in 1987. The story-poem chosen for this anthology is Cavalcante's most famous and the most successful in a commercial sense with total sales of nearly one-half million copies over the years. Cavalcante told of an especially difficult time in his life, the 1960s in the northeastern state of Bahia, when he made a meager living by traveling into the backlands of the Northeast with two suitcases full of cordelian poems, but with only one title -- "The girl ..."! So it was that Rodolfo C. Cavalcante frequented the small town markets and fairs in the dry, hot, dusty backlands and sustained a large family for several years as a traveling cordelian poet.

Cavalcante has many other titles similar to "The girl ...," and there is no doubt that the success of this single cordelian poem engendered many efforts to repeat its success. Aside from writing this type of cordelian poem, Cavalcante stood out amongst colleagues over the years in his cordelian "reporting" of the principal events of the times, including Brazilian politics. Conservative to a fault, enemy of a Marxism that he saw as a true threat to the political health of Brazil, [44] Rodolfo defended dictators, among them, the most famous of Brazilian political history, President Getúlio Vargas who governed from his "New State" in the 1930s and 1940s, was expulsed from power by the military in 1945, but returned to power as the "great democrat" in the elections of 1950.

---

43 Cavalcante's life and writings attracted this writer since the middle of the 1960s, and I dedicated a book to him and his works: The Presence of Rodolfo Coelho Cavalcante in the Modern 'Literatura de Cordel' [A Presença de Rodolfo Coelho Cavalcante na Moderna Literatura de Cordel] (Rio de Janeiro: Nova Fronteira Editora-Fundação Casa de Rui Barbosa, 1987).

44 Cavalcante's aversion to Marxism was not only ideological. He told us of an incident in Maceió, Alagoas State, when he refused to praise in verse (the common custom of a paid political poem in which the poet praised his political benefactor) a candidate of the Communist Party. Subsequently he was physically attacked by thugs hired by the same politician and was thrown into a canal to drown. Since that moment the poet became a declared enemy of "atheistic communism" in life and verse.

The poet years later would defend the military regime of 1964 to 1985 deemed a dictatorship by almost all Brazilians, especially in his personal campaign against the ravages of the immorality of the 1960s.

Aside from his poetry, Rodolfo was also the self-declared leader of the humble poets of "cordel" from 1955 until his death in 1987 and a popular journalist with his own tabloid style newspaper since the 1940s. He died poor, still battling for the economic survival of his family and of the poets of "cordel" as well. He was a fine public speaker who declaimed his poems in the marketplace with flair and elegance, perhaps as a result of his younger days as a "secretary of publicity" and "crier" for tiny circuses that traveled the Northeast and then as "propagandist" or "crier" for small shops during his youth in Alagoas. He was, in sum, one of the most colorful of the poets of modern "cordel."

"The Girl Who Beat Up Her mother and Was Turned into a Dog."	"A Moça Que Bateu na Mãe e Virou Cachorra."
Rodolfo Coelho Cavalcante	Rodolfo Coelho Cavalcante

I'm going to tell yet another "example" Which really took place Since all unbelieving souls Live in darkness, Have empty hearts, And condemn religion With a total lack of belief.	Vou contar mais um exemplo Dentro da realidade Pois toda alma descrente Vive na obscuridade, Tem um vácuo coração Condena a Religião Com toda incredulidade.
Better to be a sincere atheist Then a bad religious person There are many people who live Making fun of the All Powerful Thus blaspheming In the beginning scoffing at God And finally, always meeting a bad end.	Antes um atéu sincero Do que um mau religioso Tem muita gente que vive Zombando do Poderoso E assim a profanar Começa de Deus zombar Termina sempre inditoso.

Helen Matias was	Helena Matias era
The daughter of a religious mother,	Filha de uma religiosa,
Dona Matilde – her mother	Dona Matilde – a mãe dela
A holy and virtuous soul,	Alma santa e virtuosa,
But Helen to the contrary	Porém ela ao contrário
Was a false relic	Era um falso relicário
A really vain type.	Tipo mesmo vaidosa.
In Canindé, Ceará[45]	Em Canindé, Ceará
This narration took place	Deu-se esta narração
Helen Matias Borges	Helena Matias Borges
Was changed into a dog,	Foi transformada em um cão,
Because of her wicked tongue	Por sua língua ferina
Her fate changed her	Transformou a sua sina
Into a most horrible dragon!	Num mais horrível dragão!
Helen every once in awhile	Helena de vez em quando
Would beat up her mother,	Dava surra na mãe dela,
When the old lady complained	Quando a velha reclamava
About such an evil deed, Helen	Um qualquer mal feito, ela
With this grew even angrier,	Com isso se aborrecia,
Beating the poor old lady more,	Na pobre velha batia,
Until Helen was turned into a dog.	Até que virou cadela.
On Good Friday of Holy Week	Era u'a Sexta-Feira Santa
Known then as the Passion	Conhecida da Paixão,
Helen said to her mother:	Helena disse a mãe dela:
-- I'll be turned into a dog	-- Quero me virar num cão
If this so-called GOOD FRIDAY	Se esta tal SEXTA-FEIRA
Of HOLY WEEK isn't just foolishness	Da PAIXAO não é besteira
Of our religion!	Da nossa Religião!
-- Don't say that, my daughter	-- Não diga isso, minha filha
That's the art of the Anti-Christ,	Que é arte do Anti-Cristo,
Good Friday of Holy Week	Sexta-feira da Paixão
Recalls the blood of Christ,	Relembra o sangue de Cristo,
That was shed for us!	Que por nós foi derramado!
Helen said: that's a joke.	Disse Helena: Isto é gozado.
It's all rubbish; that's clear!	Tudo é bobagen, está visto.

---

[45] Canindé, Ceará, is a well-known place of religious pilgrimage in Brazil's Northeast, with a basilica dedicated to St. Francis of Assisi. By placing the beginning of his story in such a place, the poet knew his readers would immediately be drawn into the narrative.

-- Helen, I pray to God
Don't make fun of the Savior!
-- Hey Mom, a full stomach
Is something a lot better ...
All that stuff is silliness:
Christ, Priests, God, Images,
For me, they're worth nothing!

-- At the hour we're born
We bawl right away to eat ...
Hey I want to eat salted jerkey
Only if I heard God Himself say:
"Helen, don't eat this!"
I don't even know Christ,
I never saw him, nor can I believe!

When Matilde, her mother
Began to counsel Helen,
She slapped her
Without pity, without mercy
So that the old lady fell down crying
And began praying to God
In the form of a curse, and not a small one.

-- I have faith, damnable daughter,
In the Holy Virgin Mary,
In all the saints in heaven,
That one day you will be changed
Into an indolent dog,
So you learn, you serpent,
That a mother must be respected!

I have faith in that Saint
Who died to save us,
That in the body of a dog
Very soon you will be changed ...
May your heart not be surprised ...
On the face of your mother
You will look never more!

-- Helena, por Deus te peço
Não zombes do Salvador!
--Minha mãe, barriga cheia
É algo superior ...
Tudo isso são bobagens:
Cristo, Padres, Deus, Imagens,
Para mim não têm valor!

--Na hora que a gente nasce
Chora logo p'ra comer ...
Eu quero comer JABA[46]
Só se eu ouvisse Deus dizer:
"Helena, não coma isto!"
Eu não conheço Cristo,
Nunca o vi, nem posso crer!

Quando Matilde, a mãe dela
Foi aconselhar Helena,
Esta deu-lhe uma bofetada
Sem piedade, sem pena
Que a velha caiu chorando
E a Deus foi suplicando
Numa praga, não pequena.

-- Tenho fé, filha maldita,
Na Santa Virgem Maria,
Em todos os santos do Céu,
Que hás de virar um dia
Numa cachorra, indolente,
Para saberes, serpente,
Se uma mãe não tem valia.

Tenho fé naquele Santo
Que morreu pra nos salvar,
Que num corpo de cachorra
Brevemente hás de virar ...
Teu coração não estranhe ...
No rosto de tua mãe
Nunca mais tu hás de dar!

---

46 "Jaba," a word of Tupí origin, is jerky or the salted meat of the backlands, fresh meat that is preserved with salt and dried in the sun, one of the staples of backlands' diet.

Mark J. Curran

A burst of wind	Uma rajada de vento
Came like a hurricane	Passou feito um furacão
A bolt of lightning struck close by	Um raio caiu bem perto
With the reverberation of the thunder …	Com o ribombar do trovão …
All the earth trembled;	Toda a terra tremeu;
And then the sun was hidden	Logo o sol se escondeu
For two seconds in space.	Dois segundos na amplidão.
Helena always joking	Helena sempre a zombar
Set at eating the meat,	Se pôs a carne a comer,
Seeing her mother crying,	Vendo a mãe dela chorando,
She wanted to beat her even more,	Queria mais lhe bater,
But Divine Justice	Mas a Justiça Divina
Showed the murderous daughter	Mostrou a filha assassina
Its supreme power!	O seu Supremo Poder!
Helena continued	Helena continuava
Her blasphemous ways	Fazendo profanação
She ate more out of spite	Comeu mais por despeito
That JERKY FROM THE BACKLANDS	A tal CARNE DO SERTAO
And she said to her mother:	E disse para a mãe dela:
"May God turn me into a dog	"Deus me vire numa cadela
That is, if He even exists!"	Se é que Ele existe ou não!"
When Helena said this	Quando Helena disse isto
Her entire face was changed,	O rosto todo mudou,
With a tail like that of a dog	E cauda como cadela
The girl was transformed …	A moça se transformou …
A horrifying dog	Uma cachorra horrorosa
Foaming at the mouth, furious	Espumando e furiosa
She remained at that moment.	Naquela hora ficou.
She had a human's head	Tinha a cabeça de gente
With her former, normal features	Com a mesma feição dela
But her body up to the tail	Mas do corpo até a cauda
Was that of a horrifying dog …	Era uma horrível cadela …
Thus Helen was punished,	Foi Helena castigada,
A daughter facing damnation	Uma filha amaldiçoada
The punishment fell on her.	O castigo pegou nela.

Dona Matilde looking upon	Dona Matilde ali vendo
That horrifying creature	Aquele caso horroroso
Walked to the local church	Dirigiu-se pra Matriz
With a heavy heart	Com o coração pesaroso
She recounted all to the local priest	Contou ao Padre local
Of the Holy Cathedral	Da Excelsa Catedral
Of glorious St. Francis!	São Francisco glorioso!
There all around Canindê	Ali dentro do Canindê
The news was going round	A notícia se espalhou
The dog by this time	A cachorra nesta hora
Had mangled many people,	Muita gente estraçalhou,
No one could kill it	Ninguém a pôde matar
They drew near to catch it	Cercaram para pegar
But no one succeeded.	Porém ninguén a pegou.
The rabid animal,	O animal furioso,
Horrible, possessed,	Horrível, endemoniado,
Moved on to Pernambuco	Passou para Pernambuco
Like a starving wolf…	Feito um lobo esfomeado…
It was seen in Juazeiro	Foi vista em Juazeiro
Almost killing a religious pilgrim	Quase matando um romeiro
Of Holy Father Cícero![47]	Do Padre Cícero sagrado!

---

[47] Juazeiro, Ceará, originally a tiny town in the fertile region of the Cariri, was converted into the most famous site of religious pilgrimage by the humble outlanders of the Northeast, thanks to Father Cícero Romão Batista (1844-1934). Cícero was the priest of Juazeiro and a miracle was attributed to him when upon the occasion of celebrating mass and distributing Holy Communion, the host was turned to blood in the mouth of one of the women who attended that day. Cícero was provisionally suspended from priestly duties while an investigation into the matter could take place, but his fame grew exponentially, curiously not so much because of the "miracle," but due to his reputation in the entire area as a good man of the cloth and his unlimited charity to the poor. The result is that he became the object of the greatest religious pilgrimage of the Northeast and an important protagonist in the cordelian literature.

Mark J. Curran

Crato, Cedro, Missão Velha,[48]	Crato, Cedro, Missão Velha,
In the State of Ceará …	No Estado de Ceará …
She went as far as Campo Maior,	Foi até Campo Maior,
Passing by Tianguá	Passou por Tianguá
Wounding a man in Viçosa	Feriu um homem em Viçosa,
This terrifying dog	Esta cadela horrorosa
Made life miserable for many.	Fez muitas misérias lá.
Serrinha, Bonfim, as far as Feira	Serrinha, Bonfim, até Feira
The dog has been seen there.	Já foi vista a tal cadela.
It almost killed a child	Quase mata uma criança
In the city of Petrolina,	Na cidade Petrolina,
It returned again to Cocal	Voltou de novo a Cocal
And on the road to Sobral	E na Estrada de Sobral
It bit a poor little girl.	Mordeu u'a pobre menina.
In January of this year,	Em janeiro deste ano,
The dog was in Bahia,	Ela esteve na Bahia,
It passed right by Tucano,	Passou perto de Tucano,
Then went down to Santa Luzia,	Desceu a Santa Luzia,
It went by Jacuípe,	Passou pelo Jacuípe,
Then it arrived in Sergipe	Depois chegou em Sergipe
Creating the same agonies.	Fazendo a mesma agonia.
They say it always attacks	Dizem que ela sempre ataca
Just before nightfall,	Quando a noitinha aparece,
It has the head of a girl,	Tem cabeça de moça,
Thusly it suffers in this world,	Assim no mundo padece,
Having the body of a dog,	Tendo o corpo de cachorra,
It lives in a gloomy dungeon,	Vive ela numa masmorra,
And never forgets its mother.	Da mãe dela não se esquece.

---

48 What follows is an interesting technique of many of the poets of "cordel:" the mention of many familiar place names of towns known throughout the Northeast, in many cases, places visited by the poet on market day. The intention was to call each place to the attention of the potential reader, a technique no different from that of the singer or comedian of today of always including a warm word to the dwellers of the town where he is performing. Clearly the idea was to increase sales. Rodolfo Coelho Cavalcante used it often to sell his poems during his travels of forty years throughout the interior of the Northeast.

It went twice	Duas vezes que ela foi
To the zone of the backlands	A zona do seu sertão
To ask of its mother	Para pedir a mãe dela
Her holy pardon,	Seu sacrossanto perdão,
And it is seen with a priest	Mas, com um "Padre" se avista
And he says she must resist	E diz que ela resista
If she wants to have salvation.	Se quer ter a salvação.
The girl's penance	A penitência da moça
Is to suffer for twenty years,	É vinte anos sofrendo,
And that is why she suffers,	Por isso que ela padece,
Whining, cursing herself,	Uivando, se maldizendo,
Attacking people by night,	Pegando de noite gente,
It's a fierce dog	É uma cachorra valente
Which has been appearing for years.	Que há anos vem aparecendo.
Some say that she already was	Afirmam que ela já foi
Disenchanted a short while ago,	Há pouco desencantada,
But, that's just gossip, since already	Mas, é boato, pois, já
Just this month she was seen	Neste mês foi avistada
In the backlands near Agua-Bela	No sertão de Agua Bela
And it's the same dog	E é a mesma cadela
That was transformed in Ceará.	Do Ceará encantada.
I wrote another cordel book	Outro livro escrevi
Telling Helen's story,	Contando a história de Helena,
But it wasn't like this one,	Mas, não era como esta,
The other one was smaller,	Sendo a outra mais pequena,
This one I wrote now,	Esta agora que escrevi
Because I ran into her mother	Porque a mãe dela eu vi
Over there in Santa Madalena.	Lá em Santa Madalena.
The girl's uncle told me	Contou-me um tio da moça
That this is a true story[49]	Que essa história é patente
It remains as an example for other girls	Fica um exemplo pras outras

[49] The poet had much to say of writing examples, particularly since he claimed that fifty per cent of his total production was this type of poem. He was proud that his poems always carried a moral message, a "good" message for his readers. But as to the often outlandish details of the examples, he went so far as to call such stories "foolishness," but apparently was not so bothered by the income they provided to him. At the same time he swore that the readers of "cordel" in the backlands truly believed them. This explains the attempt at realism in recounting the very real places where the dog was seen, the encounter with the mother and the uncle's statement in the poem. "Cordel" is meant to entertain first of all, but also to teach and inform, and the poet was a master of the genre.

Mark J. Curran

To take a look at themselves ...	Se mirarem em sua frente ...
She who does not respect her mother	Quem uma mãe não respeita
That person is subject ...	A pessoa está sujeita
To suffer bitterly.	A sofrer amargamente.
So I counsel all young ladies:	A toda moça aconselho:
-- Use good sense,	-- Tenha juízo bastante,
"A mother is for 100 children"	"Uma mãe é pra cem filhos"
So says the important adage,	Diz o adagio importante,
Making fun of your mother is bad luck	Zombar da mãe é espeto
He who wrote this "folheto."	Quem escreveu o folheto
Was RODOLFO CAVALCANTE.	Foi RODOLFO CAVALCANTE.
End	Fim

Cover of the story-poem "Story of Mariquinha and José de Sousa Leão" by João Ferreira de Lima

4.

"Story of Mariquinha and José de Sousa Leão"
"História de Mariquinha e José de Sousa Leão"
João Ferreira de Lima

This story-poem was chosen by the author only after much thought; the reason is it must represent in this necessarily limited anthology the largest and perhaps most entertaining cycle of all the "literatura de cordel," the heroic. The author wavered between choosing perhaps the most famous story of "cordel, "The Mysterious Peacock" [O Pavão Misterioso] or "The Mysterious Bull" [O Boi Misterioso] or the story-poem of Charlemagne and His Twelve Knights, before settling on "Mariquinha and José de Sousa Leão" because not only does the the latter story-poem have vestiges of the European heroic poem, but really is its assimilated, Brazilian version employing the archetypes of both the Northeastern bandit and brave outlander.

This "story" is really one of the "romances" [romances] or long, narrative poems of the Brazilian "literatura de cordel." It has less than the customary 32 pages, that is, 24, but it follows the thematc scheme and possesses the primarily heroic tone of the "romance" from "cordel." And so it is that the scholars of "cordel" dub it a "traditional romance." It was composed by João Ferreira de Lima from the town of São José do Egito in the state of Pernambuco. Ferreira de Lima lived from 1907 to 1973 and besides being a cordelian poet he also plied the trade of astrologer, and he published the most popular almanac in all the Northeast from 1935 to 1972: "The Almanac of Pernambuco" [O Almanaque de Pernambuco].

The poem really fits into several "cycles" or thematic divisions of "cordel": it is a long, narrative poem of love, great suffering, challenges, battles and final victory for the lovers. But aside from this theme dear to old "cordel," it is a poem about bravery and brave heroes of the Northeast; its hero is a variant of the epic hero, a fierce Brazilian from the backlands. And it has something of the cycle of the northeastern bandit [o cangaceiro]. "Mariquinha and José de Sousa Leão" therefore is a traditional long narrative with a hero and heroine in a tremendous battle against Evil, personified in this case in the ferocious father of the girl, Captain Oliveiros.

The story-poem without doubt represents a romance assimilated to the Northeast because the theme of great love between hero and heroine is old and important in the popular stories from the Iberian Peninsula. But in the Brazilian "cordel," the hero is no longer a prince but a cowboy from the Northeast; the heroine is not a princess or daughter of the king or a cruel and despotic duke, but the daughter of a powerful landholder of the backlands. So this poem has in common with other romances like The Valiant Vilela [O Valente Vilela] or Zezinho and Mariquinha [Zezinho e Mariquinha] the fact that it is based on European themes but now assimilated to Brazil. It shows the influence of another popular story-poem of the era, an older story written by the master of old cordel, Leandro Gomes de Barros, Alonso and Marina; in fact it cites verses by Leandro in the first pages of the story.

The same formula of The Story of Mariquinha and José de Sousa Leão was redone by the same author years later when he composed his Romance of José de Sousa Leão [Romance de José de Sousa Leão], the latter with a setting in Argentina and Bolivia. And the same theme is seen often in the erudite literature of Brazil's Northeast, especially in Jorge Amado's novel Tereza Batista Tired of War [Tereza Batista Cansada de Guerra] when the female protagonist has a heroic battle against a vile landholder of the backlands, a novel based directly and consciously on the "literatura de cordel."[50]

The success of this story-poem was such that it was reprinted by the largest publisher of "cordel' in the South of Brazil, the Editora Luzeiro Lmtd. in São Paulo. So the story-poem not only was not lost over time, but became available to northeastern migrants now living in that city as well as the outlets of Editora Luzeiro in all the Northeast and North of Brazil.

---

50 See our monograph Jorge Amado e a Literatura de Cordel (Salvador da Bahia: Fundação Cultural do Estado da Bahia – Fundação Casa Rui Barbosa, 1981).

"The Story of Mariquinha and José de Sousa Leão"
João Ferreira de Lima

In this story one sees
The power that love has
And how much God helps
The man who thinks well
Who is of strong will
Only black falseness
Never served anyone well.

The force that love has
No one can overcome it
It gives courage to the weak man
Who loses his fear of death
Becomes fast as the wind
Creates wounds on the inside
That one from the outside never sees.

In the last century
José de Sousa Leão
Was a horse trader and lived
In the interior of the backlands
An elegant young man
He was always on the move
Making deals in his trade.

José de Sousa Leão
Was living in Ceará State
When there was a big drought
José migrated from there[51]
He lost any profit he had made
And he came to Pernambuco[52]
To try life out this way.

"História de Mariquinha e José de Sousa Leão"
João Ferreira de Lima

Nesta história se ve
A força que o amor te
E Deus o quanto ajuda
Ao homem que pensa ben
Tendo força de vontade
Só a negra falsidade
Nunca valeu a ninguém.

A força que o amor tem
Não há quem possa vencer
Dá coragem ao homem fraco
Perde o medo de morrer.
Fica veloz como o vento.
Cria ferida por dentro
Quem está fora não ver.

No século próximo passado
José de Sousa Leão
Era almocreve e morava
No interior do sertão
Rapaz de tipo elegante
Andava sempre ambulante
Na sua especulação.

José de Sousa Leão
Morava no Ceará
Numa seca muito grande
José emigrou de lá
Perdeu o que tinha lucro
Veio para o Pernambuco
Remir a vida por cá.

---

51 Ceará state is located in one of the traditionally hardest hit areas when the major droughts come to the Northeast.
52 Pernambuco is south and east of Ceará and as one travels toward the Atlantic the soil turns richer with abundant water.

Mark J. Curran

José checked out the south area	José percorreu o sul
Without finding a new job	Sem achar colocação
They told him: Over yonder is	Lhe disseram: Ali tem
The Captain's plantation[53]	O engenho do capitão
They pointed toward it [saying]	Apontaram com o dedo
If you are not afraid	Se o senhor não tem medo
The man is incredibly valiant.	O homem é valentão.
José said, I'll go there	José disse: eu vou lá
And he headed in that direction	E seguiu na direção
An old man who was nearby told him:	Um velho ainda lhe disse:
Don't go there my friend	Não vá lá meu cidadão
I'm giving you this advice	Dou-lhe este parecer
It hurts me to even say	Faz pena até se dizer
Who that captain is.	Quem é esse capitão.
The old man said; my boy	O velho disse: Meu moço
You better keep this secret	Você me guarde o segredo
Our captain here	Nosso capitão aqui
Kills people for the fun of it	Mata gente por brinquedo
He has no pity on anyone	Não tem dó de ninguém
More than one hundred have been buried	Já entrou mais de cem
Over there in that bunch of trees.	Dentro aquele arvoredo.
José responded: old man	José respondeu: meu velho
That all depends on luck	Isso depende de sorte
A man in order to live	O homem para viver
Needs to be strong	Precisa que seja forte
Not fear danger	Não tema revolução
And if he needs to	E se houver precisão
Risk life or death.	Troque a vida pela morte.
José in that moment	José nessa ocasião
Said goodbye and left	Disse adeus e foi embora
The old man said: May you go	O velho disse: Vai-te
With God and Our Lady	Com Deus e Nossa Senhora
José left trailing his herd	José saiu tangendo
The old man saying behind him:	O velho ficou dizendo:
That one's a dead man in no time.	Ele é morto sem demora.

53 The strophe refers to the fame of the arch-type powerful man of the backlands: the big landholder who is at the same time strong and cruel and who possesses the rank, legitimate or not, of colonel or captain in the National Guard. This figure is based on the famous "colonelism" [coronelismo] of the Northeast (a Brazilian variation of "caciquismo," the rule of the local political chief in Spanish America).

José arrived at the plantation	José chegou no engenho
With all of his string of horses	Com sua cavalaria
He greeted everyone	Cumprimentou a todos
With the greatest courtesy	Com a maior cortesia
He said in a well-mannered way	Disse com educação
Good afternoon, Captain	Boa tarde capitão
How are you doing, sir?	Como vai vossa senhora?
The arrogant captain	O capitão orgulhoso
Not even deigning to look at José	Nem para José olhou
After ten or twelve minutes	Com dez ou doze minutos
The Captain turned to him	O capitão se virou
Determining one more man's destiny	Resolveu outro destino
With an assassin's look	Com cara de assassino
He spoke in this manner:	Por esta forma falou:
Mister, where do you come from?	De onde vem o senhor?
And what do you want here?	E o que quer por aqui?
You insolent vagabond	Atrevido vagabundo
The road out is that way	O caminho é por ali
José de Sousa Leão	José de Sousa Leão
Said: I'm a citizen	Disse: Eu sou cidadão
Resident of the Cariri.[54]	Morador do Cariri.
I left my homeland	E saí de minha terra
Due to the drought going on up there	Devido a seca que há
I've got all my documents	Tenho os meus documentos
I'm a son of Ceará	Sou filho do Ceará
I'm wandering here in this hell	Ando aqui neste inferno
But when winter rains come[55]	Mas quando houver inverno
I'll return there.	Eu torno volta p'ra lá.

---

54 Cariri is the region in the south of Ceará state known from the Indians of the same name, and more recently, by the towns of Crato and Juazeiro do Norte, the land of Father Cícero, the most important personage of the religious cycle of "cordel."

55 An eternal and legendary topic of the Northeast: the migrant who leaves his land (generally for Rio de Janeiro or São Paulo in the South) because of the terrible droughts, but feels nostalgia [saudades] for his homeland and wants to return home when the much awaited rains arrive.

The captain had determined	O capitão conheceu
José's character	A sua disposição
He offered him a job	Lhe ofereceu serviço
At that very moment	Nessa mesma ocasião
Before José could say anything	Antes que José falasse
He ordered him to bunk	Mandou ele arranchar-se
In a small shack.	Num pequeno barracão.
The captain said: José	O capitão disse: José
I'm not fooling around with you	Não lhe trago enganado
Anyone not toeing the line	Quem não andar direito
I'll have his throat slit	Eu mando matar sangrando
José said: Very well	José disse: Muito bem
I'm aware that you have	Eu sei que o senhor tem
That sacred right.[56]	O seu direito sagrado.
The captain got up	O capitão levantou-se
And said: Let's go over there	E disse: Vamos ali
He took him to a clearing	Levou ele a uma quinta
And showed him	E mostrou-lhe de por si
A man who was tied up	Um homem lá amarrado
He said: His throat's going to be slit.	Disse: Vai morrer sangrado
No one here can save him.	Ninguém o salva daqui.
The grave was already dug	A sepultura aberta
The poor man meeting his end	O pobre se lastimando
There were four hired gunmen there	Com quatro cabras ali
Waiting for the boss's orders	Pelo patrão esperando
The captain with a knife	O capitão com um punhal
At that fatal moment	Nesse momento fatal
Proceeded to cut his throat.	Foi logo ao pobre sangrando.
And after he killed him	E depois que matou ele
He gave the order: bury him!	Deu ordem: Vão sepultar!
And he said to José:	E disse para José:
Now, get to work	Agora vá trabalhar
Any lack of respect	Se faltar com o respeito
That's the way you'll die.	Irá morrer desse jeito
And there' no one to complain to.	Não tem de quem se queixar.

---

[56] It's curious that the total domination by the landholder is considered here a "sacred right" by our hero, a matter of debate by researchers of the "cordel."

José went to work He said: I see how it is The Captain began to appreciate José's work But he was fooled Because this time he would see That the shoe was on the other foot.	José foi trabalhar Disse: Já sei como é O capitão agradou-se Do trabalho de José Porém ele se enganou Que dessa vez encontrou Forma que deu no seu pé.
José said: Captain I don't like offending anyone I'm happy to serve you I know you pay well But as my father said: Sometimes things don't turn out The way you think they should.	José disse: Capitão Eu não gosto de ofensa Estou pronto p'ra servi-lo Sei que o senhor compensa Porém dizia meu pai: As vezes as cousas não sai Do jeito que a gente pensa.
The next day José Took his horses To the determined place And he worked extremely well According to his modest upbringing Even the captain Was surprised and and took notice.	No outro dia José Seus cavalos carregou No ponto determinado Bem direito trabalhou Como modesto educação Até mesmo o capitão Daquilo se admirou.
After a month and a few days That José had been working José was in good standing And the captain conversed regularly with him Finding his work well done Happy and well satisfied He now criticized and joked.	Com um mês e poucos dias Que José trabalhava José estava benquisto Já o capitão conversava Achando tudo bem feito Muito alegre e satisfeito Já criticava e zombava.
One day the captain said: José, let's go over to the house I'd like you to come today To have a cup of coffee with me Mariquinha[57] has a request For you to buy something for her Let's find out what it is.	Um dia o capitão disse: Vamos lá em casa José Quero que tu vá hoje Tomar comigo um café Mariquinha quer mandar Encomendar p'ra comprar Vamos saber o que é.

---

[57] The young lady-heroine is the symbol from the old popular tradition -- the only daughter of the powerful landholder who is destined to fall in love with the young man of humble background who in turn will have to face the anger of the powerful father. It is an eternal theme of world folklore.

José was drinking coffee	José tomando café
In the dining room	Na sala da refeição
Mariquinha when she saw	Mariquinha quando viu
José de Sousa Leão	José de Sousa Leão
Her soul filled with happiness	Sua alma teve alegria
A lightning bolt of sympathy	Um raio de simpatia
Struck her heart.	Atingiu-lhe o coração.
Mariquinha came into the room	Mariquinha saiu fora
Smiling, said hello to José	Sorrindo lhe deu bom dia
In a loving way	Fez um sinal de namoro
It was a very pleasant smile	Um riso de simpatia
Of someone with nothing to hide	Como quem não tem mistério
José remained very serious	José ficou muito serio
Pretending he did not see it.	Fez de conta que não via.
Mariquinha very quickly	Mariquinha acelerada
Came on tiptoe	Vinha na ponta do pé
And from out in the hallway	E de lá no corredor
She winked at José	Piscava o olho a José
Finding the young man handsome	Achando lindo o moço
As to what happened during dinner	O que passou no almoço
The captain never caught on.	O capitão não deu fé.
José said: Captain	José disse: Capitão
I'll take care of her request	Vou fazer o seu mandado
He left and came back quickly	Foi e veio com urgência
Bringing everything as planned.	Trouxe tudo de agrado.
Fearing bad fortune	Temendo a sorte mesquinha
Mariquinha's attraction to him	O namoro de Mariquinha
Left quite an impression on him.	Deixou-lhe impressionado.
After that Mariquinha	Mariquinha depois disso
Wrote a secret note[58]	Fez um bilhete escondido
To José de Sousa Leão	Para José de Sousa Leão
Hiding her true intention	Suavisando o sentido
She said to her father with affection:	Disse ao velho com afeto:
Daddy, there's one thing lacking	Papai falta um objeto
Something I had forgotten about.	Que eu tinha esquecido.

---

58 The famous secret love note or letter from the dramatic tradition of the Spanish drama of Lope de Vega also plays a part in this popular folk drama of Northeast Brazil. In the Spanish romantic dramas, the secret love letters are so emotionally powerful that they burn the young ladies' hands!

Mariquinha said: Daddy When José comes by again I have another item For him to buy for me A lie; it was a letter Saying: this is Mariquinha And I was born to love you.	Mariquinha disse: Papai Quando seu José passar Eu tenho outra encomenda Para ele me comprar Mentira; era uma cartinha Dizendo: Sou Mariquinha Nasci para te amar.
The captain said: José Mariquinha didn't remember One item on the list Therefore you didn't buy it It was not written on the paper But it's Mariquinha who knows The item that was missing.	O capitão disse: José Mariquinha não se lembrou De botar uma encomenda Por isso tu não comprou O rol escrito não tinha Quem sabe é Mariquinha O objeto que faltou.
José hitched his horse To the side of the big gate Mariquinha came with a big smile With a note in her hand Saying, José, understand please Bring me this item I really need it.	José botou o cavalo Pelo lado do portão Mariquinha veio sorrindo Com um bilhete na mão Dizendo: José entenda Me traga esta encomenda Que eu tenho precisão.
José went on ahead Remembered and took a look This is what the note said: I was born to love you I give you my heart José de Sousa Leão Take pity on my pain.	José chegou adiante Lembrou-se e foi olhar O bilhete dizia assim: Eu nasci p'ra te amar Lhe entrego meu coração José de Sousa Leão Tenhas dó do meu penar.
The young men around here Don't ask for me in marriage They all fear my father And I live with this suffering Without love and attention And my father is at fault For this my suffering.	Os rapazes desta terra Não me pedem em casamento. Todos temem a meu pai Vivo neste sofrimento Sem carinho e sem agrado Meu pai é que é culpado Deste meu padecimento.

José let out a groan	José soltou um gemido
And his semblance changed	Fez o semblante mudado
The others asked him:	Os outros lhe perguntaram:
Are you getting sick?	Você está adoentado?
José rubbed his wrist	José apalpou o pulso
And said: I get worked up sometimes	Disse: Isso é um soluço
That just happens to me.	Que eu tenho acostumado.
José said to himself:	José dizia consigo:
Can this be my luck?	Que sorte é esta minha?
Unlucky is he who does not die	Desgraçado é quem não morre
For the love of Mariquinha	Pelo amor de Mariquinha
But with my strong and firm character	Com meu gênio rijo e forte
I'll risk life and death	Troco a vida pela morte
Facing evil fortune.	Chegando a sorte mesquinha.
José wrote a note	José escreveu um bilhete
With all due attention	Com dedicada atenção
Be confident in my strength	Se confia em meu poder
I swear with all my heart	Eu juro em meu coração
By our God of Israel	Por nosso Deus de Israel
I am your faithful lover	Sou teu amado fiel
José de Sousa Leão.	José de Sousa Leão.
José continued, saying,	José prosseguiu dizendo
In this way:	Por esta forma assim:
In one week's time	De hoje a oito dias
Be waiting for me	Você espere por mim
I'll be there in an instant	Que eu chego num instante
A little after mid-night	De meia-noite em diante
At the gate of the garden.	Lá no portão do jardim.
I'm going to sell my horses to your father	Vendo os cavalos a seu pai
And I'll say that I am leaving	E digo que vou embora
I'll keep my best horse	Deixo o cavalo melhor
To take you my lady away[59]	Para levar a senhora
To the lands of Cariri	P'ras zonas do Cariri
And I want to leave here	E quero sair daqui
From mid-night to one a.m.	De meia-noite a uma hora.

---

[59] This is the famous carrying off of the heroine of "cordel:" its most famous case was when Lampião the infamous bandit hero took away his lover Maria Bonita, she seated behind him on the back of his horse. The scene also became an important theme depicted in the famous clay dolls [bonecos de barro] of the Northeast's rural markets in the 1960s and 1970s, products of popular artisans.

No one should know about this	Não convém que ninguém saiba
And be careful with the Captain	Cuidado no capitão
After I leave here	Depois que eu sair daqui
Heading to the deep backlands	Rumar ao alto sertão
Returning would be disastrous	Minha volta é ruim
And don't let anyone try to go against me	Ninguém vá contra mim
Because he will lose in the end.	Porque perde na questão.
José feigned sickness	José fingiu-se doente
Suffering from heart trouble	Sofrendo de coração
With great consideration	Com muita benevolência
He asked the captain	Pediu para o capitão
To allow him to depart	Deixar ele ir embora
He [the captain] said to him	Qualquer hora
Is fine with me.	Está a sua disposição.
Due to the fact he was sick	Devido ele estar doente
The Captain agreed:	O capitão combinou:
Go visit your parents	Vá visitar os seus pais
José told him: I'm going	José lhe disse: Eu vou
To visit my backlands	Visitar o meu sertão
Even the Captain	Até mesmo o capitão
Shed a few tears for hm.	Lágrimas por ele botou.
José de Sousa sold	José de Sousa vendeu
Eight of the horses that he had	Oito cavalos que tinha
He got a thousand, eight hundred	Fez um mil e oitocentos
Then he said to Mariquinha:	Então disse a Mariquinha:
We can go even to the moon	Vamos até para a lua
My destiny is yours	A minha sorte é a tua
And your destiny is mine.	E a tua sorte é minha.
Capitão Oliveiros[60]	O Capitão Oliveiros
Paid him all his wages	Pagou-lhe todo ordenado
The money for the horses	O dinheiro dos cavalos
And gave him a little bit besides	E deu-lhe mais um agrado
One hundred mil-reis in cash[61]	De cem-mil reis em dinheiro
And said to one of his hired gunmen	E disse a um cangaceiro
José is an honorable man.	José é um homem inteirado.

---

60 Is it a coincidence the poet gives the captain the same name as the famous knight of France as in the classic "Charlemagne and His Seven Knights of France?" (See the reference in the "Duel between Patrick and Ignatius da Catingueira" later in this anthology.)

61 "Mil-reis" was the Brazilian monetary unit early in the 20th century; the tip is a sizable amount.

Mark J. Curran

The captain gave José	O capitão deu a José
A dagger and a long knife	Um punhal e um facão
An old grenadier	Um granadeiro velho
Which looked big as a cannon	Que parecia um canháó
-- Say to anyone who respects you	-- Tu diz a quem te venera
You were one more bloodthirsty killer	Que estavas mais uma fera
But I was a good boss.	Mas era um lindo patrão.
José said: Very good	José disse: Muito bem
I feel quite well gratified	Eu fui bem gratificado
I'm very obliged	Estou muito agradecido
And eternally thankful	Eternamente obrigado
I owe you no end of favors	Devo favores sem fim
And if you need me	E precisando de mim
Count on this your servant.	Conte com um seu criado.
The captain recognized	O capitão conheceu
That José was courageous	Que José tinha coragem
José at that moment	José durante esse tempo
Was thinking about his plan	Pensava em sua imagem
Only he and she knew	Só ele e ela sabia
Until the day would arrive	Até que chegou o dia
To begin their journey.	De seguirem a viagem.
José de Sousa possessed	José de Sousa possuía
A fine, tested horse	Um bom cavalo rodado
With fine bridle and saddle	Com arreios muito bons
He was well prepared	Estava bem preparado
With horse and arms	De cavalo e armamento
His thoughts were heroic	O seu herói pensamento
He already had made a plan.	Já tinha um plano formado.
At eleven o'clock at night	As onze horas da noite
José arrived at the gate	José chegou ao portão
Mariquinha was already there	Mariquinha já estava
With her bag in her hand	Com uma bolsa na mão
On a cobblestone stoop that was there	Numa calçada que tinha
José helped her mount up	José montou Mariquinha
They headed to the high backlands.	Rumaram ao alto sertão.

Brazil's Folk-Popular Poetry – A Literatura De Cordel

One of the ranch dogs[62]	Um cachorro da fazenda
By the name of Swordfish	Chamado de Espadarte
Accompanied José	Acompanhou José
José with the blunderbuss	José com o bacamarte
The long knife and the dagger	O facão e o punhal
Said to himself: with this animal	Disse: Com esse animal
I can fight anywhere.	Eu brigo em qualquer parte.
It was an autumn night	Era uma noite de Outono
The moon shining brightly	A lua resplandecia
And the stars shone	E as estrelas brilhavam
José de Sousa said	José de Sousa dizia
To his beloved consort:	A sua imagem adorada:
For our journey	Para a nossa jornada
Nightime is better than the day.	A noite é melhor do que o dia.
At six o'clock in the morning	As seis horas da manhã
José along with his lover	José com a sua amante
Arrived at a ranch	Saíram numa fazenda
Twenty leagues distant	Com vinte léguas distante
They drank coffee with milk	Tomaram leite e café
Mariquinha said: José	Mariquinha disse: José
Be careful, we'd better get going.	Cuidado, vamos adiante.
So then they mounted up	Se montaram depois
Continuing the same journey	Seguiram a mesma jornada
Through a strange backland	Por um sertão esquisito
Where no one was living	Onde não tinha morada
They traveled for a week	Andaram uma semana
A panther	O tigre suçuarana
Insulted them from the side of the road.	Vinha insultá-los na estrada.

---

62 The role of the faithful dog, always heroic, is important in "cordel." The most famous case is the story-poem "Story of the Dog of the Dead" by Leandro Gomes de Barros, considered by some scholars to be the most successful cordelian story-poem ever by this famous poet, with nearly one million copies sold over the decades (See Orígenes Lessa, "Literatura Popular em Versos," Anhembi, dezembro, 1955, pp. 67-71.)

They almost died of hunger	Quase que morre de fome
In the interior of the backlands	No interior do sertão
During the great crossing[63]	Numa grande travessia
Of the Espigão Mountains	Da Serra do Espigão
But God helped him	Mas Deus o auxiliou
And luckily he found	Por felicidade achou
Water in a pot hole.	Água em um caldeirão.
José from far away spotted	José de longe avistou
A boulder coming out from a cliff	O penhaso dum rochedo
And at the foot of a large mountain range	E no pé da grande serra
That had a grove of trees at its base	Continha grande arvoredo
There was a "trapiá" tree	Era um pé de trapiá
José decided to stop there	José obrigou-se ir lá
In the middle of that wilderness.	Naquele enorme degredo.
At eleven o'clock in the morning	As onze horas do dia
José prepared their meal	José fez a refeição
Two jaguars came into view	Chegaram dois canguçus
At that very time	Nessa mesma ocasião
Those jaguars came	Vinham esses canguçus
Breaking through the bamboo	Arrebentando os bambus
Appearing like dragons.	Que parecia um dragão.
One attacked José	Um partiu para José
But he very quickly	Mas ele muito ligeiro
Above the left side of the chest	Em cima do peito esquerdo
Shot it with the grenadier	Disparou-lhe o granadeiro
The big cat fell to the ground	Ele tombou e caiu
And José de Sousa smiled	José de Sousa sorriu
Just like a knight in war.	Como um homem guerreiro.

---

63 The word "travessia," "crossing" in English, is charged with meaning and emotion for the people of the backlands and in northeastern popular culture. It is associated with the heroic deed, a test of strength, courage and even the moral good. It is no coincidence that João Guimarães Rosa chose the same topic using similar words for equal purposes in his masterpiece "The Devil to Pay in the Backlands," ["Grande Sertão: Veredas"]. See Mark J. Curran, "Grande Sertão: Veredas" e a literatura de cordel" in <u>Brazil/Brasil</u> (Ano 8, n. 14, 1995), a study that garnered the Orígenes Lessa Literary Prize in Brasil in 1985.

The other one then confronted	O outro logo enfrentou
José de Sousa Leão	José de Sousa Leão
And with the first blow of its paws	Logo da primeira tapa
Tore the big knife from his hands	Tomou-lhe logo o facão
Then Mariquinha shouted:	Mariquinha aí gritou:
José, the dog is behind you	José o cachorro chegou
Take your dagger in your hand.	Segure o punhal na mão.
José pulled out the dagger	José puxou o punhal
Not even appearing angry	Fez que nem deu cavaco
The beast lunged at him	A fera partiu para ele
And José like a monkey	José como um macaco
Lightning quick in a flash	Veloz igual a giranda
Twisted his body to the side	Torceu o corpo de banda
And stabbed it under the shoulder.	Cravou-lhe bem no suvaco.
The jaguar gave a roar	O tigre deu um esturro
Which made the earth tremble	Que a terra estremeceu
The dog then bit into it	O cachorro ferrou nela
And the jaguar lost heart	E o tigre esmoreceu
José grabbed it by the tail	José pegou-lhe na cauda
Stabbing it once again	Deu-lhe outra punhalada
And the old jaguar died.	O tigre velho morreu.
José said to Mariquinha:	José disse a Mariquinha:
It's late; let's get going	É tarde vamos embora
There's not a man than can do	Mas outro homem não faz
What I did just now	A cena que fiz agora
Any time I face evil	Em qualquer ato ruim
It's enough for me to have	Basta eu ter por mim
Jesus and Our Lady by my side.	Jesus e Nossa Senhora.
José continued the journey	José seguiu a viagem
When on the next day	Quando foi no outro dia
His horse began to grow weak	Seu cavalo afracou
In another great crossing	Numa grande travessia
Now a hundred leagues distant	Já com cem léguas distante
His horse so important	O seu cavalo importante
Died and without cowardice.	Morreu e não fez covardia.

Where the horse died	Aonde o cavalo morreu
There was a country shack nearby	Perto tinha uma choupana
A mixed blood lived there	Morava nela um caboclo
By the name of Santana	Chamado de Santana
With no beard, bald and wrinkled	Sem barba, calvo e franzido
And with a stray eye	E tinha um olho fuido
And no sign of an eyelash.	Sem um sinal de pestana.
José asked the mixed blood:	José pediu ao caboclo:
I need a place here	Eu quero aqui um lugar
Where no one can see me	Aonde ninguém me veja
Where I can rest	Que eu possa descansar
Pardon the inconvenience	Desculpe eu incomodá-lo
Go buy me a horse	Vá me comprar um cavalo
Whatever it may cost.	Custe lá o que custe.
He gave him 500 in money	Deu-lhe quinhentos mil-reis
Saying: I'm trusting you	Dizendo: eu confio em ti
Buy a good horse	Compre um cavalo bom
And bring it here	Traga ele para aqui
When I'm rested up	Enquanto eu tenho descanso
I'm going to see if I can get to	Quero ver se alcanço
The lands of the Cariri.	As terras do Cariri.
The mixed blood took José	O caboclo levou José
Into a palm grove	Pra dentro dum palmeira
And he told him: stay here	E lhe disse: fique aí
And no harm will come to you	Que não lhe sucede mal
You can even go to sleep	Podem dormirem até
He asked for the money from José	Pediu dinheiro a José
And left to buy the animal.	E foi comprar o animal.
José for this journey	José para a viagem
Had money in his saddle bag	Tinha dinheiro na bolsa
Courage and the right disposition	Coragem e disposição
Robust and very strong	Robustez e muita força
To defend his wife	Pra defender sua esposa
Let's leave José de Sousa	Deixamos José de Sousa
And talk about the girl's father.[64]	Tratamos no pai da moça.

---

[64] The change of scene is an important technique of cordelian heroic poetry, inherited from the epic tradition. Such changes of scene are famous, for example, in the great antecedent to "cordel," "The Story of Charlemagne and the Twelve Knights of France."

When the day dawned	Quando o dia amanheceu
The captain went to tell	O capitão foi narrar
Of how much he missed José	A falta que José faz
How can I get along without him!	Como hei de passar!
His wife said: Mariquinha	Disse a velha: Mariquinha
Is not in her room	Não está na camarinha
You had better have someone find her.	Só mandando procurar.
Three of her dresses are missing	Faltam três vestidos dela
Her hat and her purse too	O chapéu e a bolsinha
She's not in the house	Ela em casa não está
I already looked in the kitchen	Já procurei na cozinha
I'm not understanding this ...	Não sei isto o que é ...
My husband, it had to be José	Meu velho foi José
Who carried off Mariquinha.	Que carregou Mariquinha.
The captain let out a roar	O capitão deu um urro
Which shook the two-story house	Que o sobrado estremeceu
A maid fainted	U'a ama desmaiou
A young girl fell sick	Uma moça adoeceu
The black slave became sick	A negra ficou doente
[The Captain] had a lion on a chain	Tinha um leão na corrente
That broke its locks and ran away.	Quebrou os ferros e correu.
He fired off a grenadier	Disparou um granadeiro
That shook the rocks	Que os rochedos abalaram
Twenty-five hired gunmen	Vinte e cinco cangaceiros
Arrived at the same time	Na mesma hora chegaram
Ready for action	Prontos para execução
-- What's going on Captain?	-- O que há Capitão?
They all asked at once.	Todos assim perguntaram.
Captain Oliveiros	Capitão Oliveiros
Said: the devil's on the loose	Disse: o diabo se soltou
The cowhand José de Sousa	O cabra José de Sousa
Who always worked for me	Que sempre me trabalhou
Carried off my Mariquinha	Me carregou Mariquinha
So much love I had for him	Tanto amor que eu lhe tinha
See how he repaid me.	Vejam como me pagou.

Mark J. Curran

A gunman said to him: well	Um cabra lhe disse: qual
It's nothing Captain	Não é nada capitão
Whatever you want done	O que quiser que se faça
Just give us the order, "patrón"	Nos dê as ordens patrão ...
The captain groaned	O captião deu uns ais
Saying: go after	Dizendo: sigam atrás
That thieving bastard.	Daquele cabra ladrão.
And kill that unlucky daughter	Matem aquela infeliz
And let the vultures eat her	Deixem o urubu comer
And kill José de Sousa	E matem José de Sousa
Whatever may happen	Suceda o que suceder
Don't spare either one	Não faça gosto a nenhum
An ear from each one	A orelha de cada um
That's all I want to see.	É só o que quero ver.
Five of the most perverse gunmen	Cinco cabras dos perversos
Immediately hit the trail	Seguiram pela batida
Saying: let's catch them	Dizendo: vamos pegá-los
While they rest or sleep	No descanso ou na dormida
Anywhere from here to Ceará	... Daqui para o Ceará ...
And the captain remained behind	E o capitão ficou lá
Like a fearless wild beast.	Como fera destemida.
They followed the trail	Prosseguiram o roteiro
Through the same wild crossing	Pela mesma travessia
For four days and a half	Com 4 dias e meio
And at eleven o'clock in the morning	As 11 horas do dia
Almost at the end of the week	Quase no fim da semana
They arrived at the same shack	Saíram na tal choupana
Where the mixed blood lived.	Que o caboclo residia.
They asked the mixed blood:	Perguntaram ao caboclo:
Who was it that came this way	Quem foi que passou aqui
Sometime between yesterday and now?	De ontem para hoje?
The mixed blood said: I saw them	Disse o caboclo: eu vi
They are still out there in back	E estão ali por trás
A young girl and a boy	Uma moça e um rapaz
Who are heading to the Cariri.	Que vão para o Cariri.

The mixed blood went to show them	O caboclo foi mostrá-lo
Like the false traitor he was	Como falso traiçoeiro
Saying to himself: José dies	Dizendo ele: José more
And I get to keep the money	E eu fico com o dinheiro
With this plan he showed them	Com este plano os mostrou
But the tables were turned	Mas o feitiço virou
On him.	Por cima do feitceiro.[65]
José said: Mariquinha	José disse: Mariquinha
I think we are surrounded	Creio que estamos cercados
By the Captain's gunmen	Com cabras do capitão
Get down and be careful	Se deite e tome cuidado
I'm going to face the battle	Que vou enfrentar a luta
Here inside this cave	Aqui dentro desta gruta
I'll relish the fight.	Eu brigo com entusiasmo.
The gunmen shot at him	Os cabras lhe detonaram
Five shots at a time	Cinco tiros de uma vez
José de Sousa Leão	José de Sousa Leão
Got down quickly	Deitou-se com rapidez
A tactic to avoid dying	Fez tática para não morrer
It's a pity to even hear	Faz pena ouvir-se dizer
The destruction he brought upon them.	O estrago que José fez.
José de Sousa shouted out:	José de Sousa gritou:
Open your eyes you knaves	Abram os olhos canalha
Twenty of the likes of you gunmen	Vinte cabras de vocês
Can't even do me in	Inda não me atrapalha
He leveled his grenadier at them	Disparou-lhe o granadeiro
And killed them all	Matou até o derradeiro
It was like shots from a machine gun.	Só um tiro de metralha.
The mixed blood was nearby	O caboclo estava perto
Seeing all the destruction	Vendo a destruição
He said: oh that damned José	Disse: oh José danado!
That man is the devil himself	Aquele home é o cão
There's no peace here for me	Eu aqui não fico em paz
The dog went after him	O cachorro correu atrás
And threw him to the ground.	Bateu com ele no chão.

---

[65] The last two lines of verse in Portuguese are a well-known aphorism in Brazilian Portuguese.

The miserable mixed blood	O miserável caboclo
Shouted to make you pity him	Gritava de fazer dó
José de Sousa at his throat	José de Sousa na beca
And the dog at his leg	E o cachorro no mocotó
Tearing at him from behind	Também atrás de rasgá-lo
José before killing him	José antes de matá-lo
Gave him a good thrashing.	Deu-lhe muito de cipó.
José brought the knife down	José desceu o facão
Splitting open his head	Abriu-lhe a cabeça bem
Then he said to Mariquinha:	Então disse a Mariquinha:
A knife like this is useful	Um facão assim convém
Now I'm at peace	Agora estou descansado
This damned mixed blood	Este caboclo danado
Won't be false to anyone again.	Não é mais falso a ninguém.
Mariquinha became upset	Mariquinha se vexou
Bemoaning her bad fortune	Clamando a sorte dela
José going into action	José entrar em trabalho
In a battle like that	Numa batalha daquela
Feeling for her lover	Com pena de seu amante
I thought it was interesting[66]	Eu achei interessante
What José said to her.	O que José disse a ela.
Jose said: Mariquinha	José disse: Mariquinha
Don't regret what you've done	Não queira se arrepender
He who enters the field of battle	Quem vai ao campo de luta
Loses the fear of dying	Perde o medo de morrer
I'll take on an entire batallion	Eu brigo com um batalhão
I'll even kill the Captain	Mato até o capitão
I'll make myself wretched for you.	Me desgraço por você.
Let's head right now	Nós vamos agora mesmo
To the nearest town over there	Aquela povoação
In a little while we'll be married	Casaremos com brevidade
From there we'll go to the Captain	De lá vamos ao capitão
And in the shortest time	Com a maior brevidade
For or against his will	Por gosto ou contra vontade
He will give you his blessing.	Ele lhe bota a benção.

---

[66] The text becomes more interesting with the "first person" observance of the poet.

They arrived at [the town of] San Francisco	Chegaram em São Francisco
And went directly to the church	Se dirigiram a Matriz
The sacristan ran urgently	O sacristão foi urgente
To get Father Luís	Chamar o Padre Luís
He performed the marriage	Ele fez o casamento
They received the sacrament	Receberam o sacramento
Oh! What a happy moment!	Oh! Que momento feliz!
The local sheriff asked	O delegado local perguntou
José de Sousa who he was	José de Sousa quem era
José said: I am a person	José dsse: Sou um ente
Worse than the devil himself	Pior que a besta-fera
I'm not even fit to die	Não presto nem pra morrer
The sheriff said: What?	O delegado disse: O quê?
I'm speaking the truth.	Estou falando deveras.
José de Sousa threatened him	José de Sousa ameaçou-lhe
With the business end of the grenadier	Na boca do ganadeiro
The sheriff said: I swear	O delegado disse: vote
This man is an armed bandit	Este homem é cangaceiro
The priest ran from the church	O padre correu da matriz
Astonished with fear he did not want	Assombradíssimo não quis
Any longer to take José's money.	Mais receber o dinheiro.
José de Sousa continued the journey	José de Sousa seguiu
Finding no one willing to fight him	Não achou com quem brigar
He said: I'm certain	Dizia: tenho certeza
That I'm going to kill or be killed	Que vou matar ou morrer
And if I'm not mistaken	Se o espíritu não me engana
I know that the Captain will be furious	Eu sei que o velho se dana
At the moment I arrive.	Na hora que eu chegar.
José had bought	José tinha comprado
Another riding horse	Outro cavalo passeiro
Almost as fine as the first one	Quase bom que o outro
That ran like lighting along the way	Que galgava o taboleiro
New, reigning in well, easy to ride	Moderno, brando e macio
José said to himself: I trust	José disse: eu confio
Only my grenadier.	Somente no granadeiro.

Mark J. Curran

The captain had asked for	O capitão tinha pedido
A cup of coffee	Uma xícara de café
Seated out on the terrace	Assentado na terraça
When he heard horses arriving	Quando ouviu um tropé
Coming closer to the house	De casa se aproximava
There came hurriedly drawing closer	Lá vinha urgente chegando
Mariquinha and José.	Mariquinha mais José.
José rapidly leaped	José urgente saltou
From his horse to the ground	Do seu cavalo no chão
He leveled the grenadier	Escalou o granadeiro
Straight at the captain	Em cima do capitão
Swinging it back and forth	Fazendo uma manilha
Give your daughter your blessing	Bote a benção em sua filha
Tell me if you'll do it or not.	Me diga se bota ou não.
The captain said: I'll give it	O capitão disse: eu boto
His wife said: I as well	A velha disse: eu também
They all embraced	Abraçaram-se ali todos
The captain said: good	O capitão disse: bem
The game's come to an end	Agora bateu o jogo
You're my son-in-law, I'm your father-in-law	És meu genro e eu teu sogro
Blessed be God, Amen.	Nas horas de Deus. Amém.
The captain's wife embraced José	A velha abraçou José
And shook his hand	Deu-lhe um aperto de mão
The captain also told him:	O velho também lhe disse:
There's no longer any problem	Agora não há questão
José is a decent young man	José é rapaz direto
I'm very happy	Estou muito satisfeito
We have such a valiant son-in-law.	Temos um genro valentão.
Oliveiros de Vasconcelos	Oliveiros de Vasconcelos
Was the Captain's name	Era o nome do capitão
His wife was Dalila	A sua esposa Dalila
Mary of the Immaculate Conception	Maria da Conceição
Maria Nunes Clemente	Maria Nunes Clemente
Was the wife of the valiant hero	Era a mulher do valente
José de Sousa Leão.	José de Sousa Leão.
End	Fim

Cover of the story-poem "The Sufferings of the Northeasterner Traveling to the South" by Cícero Vieira da Silva, "Mocó"

5.

"Sufferings of the Northeasterner Traveling to the South"
"Os Martírios do Nortista Viajando para o Sul"
Cícero Vieira da Silva, "Mocó"

This story-poem forms part of the large cycle in the "cordel" that treats the life of the northeastern migrant who flees his poor and arid land in search of work, money, food, and in the end, his very survival. It is one of the saddest chapters of the "cordel" of the twentieth century and the Brazilian social reality from the nineteenth century onward. The underlying reality is that a large part of Brazil's Northeast is an arid land with a scarcity of rain which suffers from periods of incredible drought which even today in the twenty-first century have no solution.

The drought of 1877 remains in the annals of the region as the greatest natural disaster of the Northeast. The result of the drought was the beginning of a migratory movement that continues yet today, a migration from the Northeast toward the most distant regions in search of a bettering of life: first to the Amazon at the end of the nineteenth century to work on rubber tree plantations, then in the twentieth century to the South to work on sugar cane or coffee plantations in the states of Rio de Janeiro and São Paulo and as laborers in construction in the same two cities.[67] Due to this wave of migration it is said today that the largest "northeastern" city in Brazil is São Paulo. The migration did not stop there; it continued with the construction of the "new" capital of Brasília from 1955 to 1960 when another contingent of migrants formed the large part of the construction workers, called "candongos"

---

[67] The "anthem of the Northeast," Luís Gonzaga's "White Wing" ["Asa Branca"] tells this story in northeastern "country" music style [forró]. But one of the most beautiful artistic creations based on the same theme is by the sophisticated composer-singer Chico Buarque de Holanda in the style of Brazilian Popular Music [MPB], of the 1960s. The song "Pedro Pedreiro" [loosely translated, "Pete the laborer"] tells the story of the northeastern migrant to Rio de Janeiro or São Paulo, the laborer who perhaps builds the mosaic rock sidewalks in much of the city or labors on skyscrapers. Pedro earns little, lives poorly and dreams of returning to his beloved Northeast.

in Brasília. And most recently, other northeastern migrants went to states in the North and West of Brazil, like Rondonia or Acre, in search of land to farm and a chance to escape hunger and even death in the old Northeast.

The odyssey was immortalized in the "cordel" in story-poems written by the migrants [retirantes] themselves, among them Cícero Vieira da Silva, author of the poem chosen for this anthology, one of many poet-migrants in Rio de Janeiro who could tell a similar story. The poets Azulão (José João dos Santos) and Apolônio Alves dos Santos are also cases in point.[68] The myth is this: the poor northeasterner suffering from hunger travels to the South in search of a job; after time, he gets a job as a menial laborer, making a substandard living. He saves a little as a construction worker on the skyscrapers of Rio and São Paulo, often living in the actual buildings he is helping to construct. But he constantly suffers from homesickness for his native lands, family and way of life, the famous "saudades" of Portuguese-Brazilian culture. He dreams of returning to the Northeast and upon receiving news of the arrival of rains to the parched lands, he departs once again with the hope of living well and happily.

But the myth more often runs up against reality: the droughts continue, the migrants keep arriving and live in the giant slums of Rio or São Paulo and do not return to the Northeast which grows, if that is possible, even poorer and with little hope of improvement in life.

Thus "cordel" documents this national "odyssey," from the days of those first migrants that always dreamed of somehow returning "home" to the Northeast to those living permanently today in Rio or São Paulo along with their children born in the South. As if hard times

---

68 Apolônio Alves dos Santos, a poet this writer grew to know well after many trips to the Northeastern Fair in Rio de Janeiro, toward the end of his life fulfilled the dream of "White Wing." He returned to the Northeast (his native state of Paraíba) to start life anew, but unhappily, things did not work out and he returned once again to Rio de Janeiro where he died a few years ago. He was driven to make the odyssey back to the Northeast by the evils of the large metropolis – violence, facing dangerous thieves on a daily basis, and life in the slums [favelas]. But he also penned one of the most positive cordelian poems extolling the virtues of life in the big southern cities for "successful" migrants.

and economics were not enough, the "northeasterner" ["pau de arara" or "parrot cage" named after the slats in the trucks used to haul them south] faced and faces yet today massive prejudice just trying to survive in the South.

The topic is a mainstay in Brazilian erudite literature as well. The most famous book is "Barren Lives" ["Vidas Secas"] by Graciliano Ramos. Also important is the incredibly beautiful and poetic "Severe Death and Life" ["Morte e Vida Severina"] by the poet João Cabral de Melo Neto and its stage and cinematic versions with music composed by a young Chico Buarque de Holanda. Such works treat the migration from the backlands to the sugar cane plantations near the fertile coast of the Northeast. A third work by the renowned Jorge Amado of Bahia, "Red Harvest" ["Seara Vermelha"] combines three of the major realities and themes of the northeast: banditry, religious fanaticism and the migration of the backlanders to the South.

However, a large and faithful part of the story is told in dozens of variations and titles in "cordel."

"The Sufferings of the Northerner[69]
Traveling to the South"
Cícero Vieira da Silva ("Mocó")

The high cost of living in the North
No living being can stand
Each day that passes
The cost of living goes up
That's why the father of the family
Faces great sacrifices.

"Os Martírios do Nortista
Viajando para o Sul"
Cícero Vieria da Silva (Mocó)

A carestia do Norte
Vivente nenhum agüenta
Cada dia que se passa
O custo de vida aumenta
Por isto pai de família
Grande sacrifício enfrenta.

---

[69] One sees in the original Portuguese texts both the terms "nortista" [northerner] and "nordestino" [northeasterner]. Although literally the "northerner" should be from Brazil's "North" – the Amazon and North, practically speaking and in the "cordel," "northerner" becomes most often synonymous with "northeasterner."

Mark J. Curran

Our North is surrounded	Nosso Norte está cercado
By immense misfortune	Por uma desgraça imensa
One part has already fallen	Uma banda já caiu
The other is on the verge of it	A outra banda está pensa
The northeasterner in the middle	E o nortista debaixo
One in the masses you read about.	Igual a massa na prensa.
Today the poor northeasterner	Hoje o pobre nordestino
Lives almost dying of hunger	Vive quase morto a fome
He works for his boss	Trabalha pra seu patrão
Not making enough even to eat	Não lucra nem o que come
He only doesn't risk robbing	Só não se arrisca roubar
To not ruin his good name.	Pra não manchar o seu nome.
Happy is he who manages	Feliz daquele que arranja
To find something to eat	Ao menos o que comer
And he who earns nothing	E o que não ganha nada
What is he going to do	O que é vai fazer
Seeing his children cradled	Vendo os filhos pendurados
In the arms of suffering?	Nos braços do padecer?
He gets up very early	Se levanta bem cedinho
Facing a horrible situation	Em péssima situação
He sees his smallest child	Vê o filhinho pequeno
Stretching out his skinny hand	Estirando a magra mão
Saying: Daddy	Dizendo: meu papaizinho
I want a piece of bread.	Quero um pedaço de pão.
How can that father possibly feel	Como não fica esse pai
Looking at his small children	Olhando pra seus filhinhos
Not being able to buy even one loaf of bread	Sem ter como que compre 1 pão
To give to his tiny kids	Pra dar aos seus garotinhos
Seeing misery take possession of	Vendo a miséria apossar-se
The fruit of his love?	Dos frutos dos seus carinhos?
Therefore he leaves the house very early	Por isto ele sai bem cedo
To see if he can find work	P'ra ver se arranja emprego
He searches so long, poor man	Procura tanto, coitado
He's about out of his mind	Que perde até o sossego
Going from door to door knocking	Batendo de porta em porta
Flitting about like the saddest bat.	Feito o mais triste morcego.

He arrives home tired at night	Chega de noite cansado
Since he walked the entire day	Pois andou o dia inteiro
Disillusioned because	Desenganado porque
He could not make any money	Não pôde arranjar dinheiro
He talks to his wife and says:	Chama a mulher e diz:
I'm going to Rio de Janeiro.	Vou para o Rio de Janeiro.
The woman says: if you go	A mulher diz: se tu fôres
Everyone will die of hunger	Vai tudo morrer de fome
At least when you are at home	Pois você estando em casa
Only on some days we don't eat.	Um dia, outro não se come
But if you travel [to the south]	E se você viajar
Then, yes, everything is lost!	Aí sim tudo se some!
The poor man says: No, woman,	Diz o pobre: não, mulher
With me being in Rio de Janeiro	Eu no Rio de Janeiro
I'll get some kind of a job right away	Arranjo logo um serviço
As a bricklayer's assistant	De servente de pedreiro
And within a month, God willing,	E com um mês Deus querendo
I will be sending you money.[70]	Eu te mandarei dinheiro.
-- You stay around here	-- Você fica por aí
Doing some odd jobs	Fazendo alguns servicinhos
Washing clothes and ironing	Lavando roupa e passando
For those neighbors of ours	Pra esses nossos vizinhos
To be able to buy at least bread	Pra comprar ao menos pão
To give to our children.	Pra dar aos nossos filhinhos.
She agrees to this	Com isto ela se conforma
So he then, this time,	E ele então desta vez
Goes to a relative's house	Vai a casa dum parente
He borrows two thousand to pay three	Toma dois contos por três
But with the obligation	Porém na obrigação
To pay it back the next month.	De mandar no outro mês.

---

[70] Perhaps one of the reasons this poem and dozens like it strike such an emotional note in this writer's mind is that my own father, a small farm wheat farmer in Kansas, was forced to live a U.S. version of the same migration after years of drought and marginal returns on the farm. My father worked part-time, then full-time as a carpenter and carpenter's assistant for a construction company in Abilene, Kansas, and then was forced to travel by bus to Florida in the winter of 1955 to do the same work to keep income flowing for the family. I don't mean to compare it in any sense to the severity of the reality of this Brazilian poem, but there are some similarities.

Mark J. Curran

He goes quickly to the ticket office	Vai depressa na agência
And buys his passage right away	Compra logo uma passagem
And returns home happily	Volta pra casa contente
He gets his things together	Arruma sua bagagem
And ends up awaiting the day	E fica esperando o dia
Of that sad journey.	Daquela triste viagem.
The ticket that he bought	A passagem que comprou
Cost a thousand seven hundred	Foi um conto e setecentos
Of the two thousand he borrowed	Dos dois contos que tomou
Only three hundred were left	Ficou somente trezentos
That's when they begin to come forth	Daí começa a surgir
His first sufferings.	Seus primeiros sofrimentos.
He quickly runs to the store	Corre depressa na venda
And buys a quantity	Compra logo uma fartura
Of salted meat and crackers	De carne seca e bolacha
Matches, tobacco and hard sugar candy	Fósforo, fumo e rapadura[71]
A quart of "Dry Goat" rum	Um cuarto de "Bode Seco"[72]
Sweet rolls and pure manioc flour.	Pão doce e farinha pura.
He picks up all that meat	Pega toda aquela carne
And places it on a spit	Enfila numa vareta
Sticks it in the coals	E sarrabulha na brasa
Until the meat turns black	Chega a carne ficar preta
Finds a pack for it	Arruma numa mochila
And throws that into his suitcase.	Depois bota na maleta.
He says goodbye to the family	Se despede da família
And blesses all the children	E abençoa os filhinhos
With a heavy heart	Com a alma pesarosa
He kisses them a thousand times	Dá-lhes milhão de beijinhos
Leaving the seed of missing them	Deixando um pé de saudades
To become the fruit of all his caring.	Na planta dos seus carinhos.[73]

---

71 "Rapadura" is a type of hardened dark sugar and molasses, in the form of a small brick, which is scraped and eaten as a dessert or a sweetener for coffee in the backlands of the Northeast.

72 "Bode Seco." We surmise via its context in the poem that this is a brand name of a type of sugar cane rum ["cachaça"] common to the Northeast.

73 The metaphor in Portuguese is a bit nebulous and difficult to translate. Our interpretation is that it is indeed clever and harkens back to the rural, telluric essence of old "cordel." The father emotionally "plants" the seed or seedling of his homesickness and deep emotions for his family that will grow into a plant, bush or even small tree of all his caring for his loved ones.

The poor guy climbs up into the truck	Se sobe o pobre no carro
And leaves waving his hand	E sai dando a mão
His children stay by the door	Os filhos ficam na porta
Feeling the separation	Sentindo a separação
Saying: there goes Daddy	Dizendo: lá vai papai
On top of the bed of the truck.	Em cima do caminhão!
The children cry at her side	Os filhos choram dum lado
The wife sobs and shouts	A mulher soluça e grita
At that sad hour	Naquela hora tristonha
When the truck honks its horn	Que o caminhão apita
And leaves, cutting through the dust	E sai cortando a poeira
Of the long, strange road.	Da longa estrada esquisita.[74]
So the poor man travels subject to	Sai o pobre recebendo
Sun, dirt, and cold rain	Sol, poeira, e chuva fria
When he passes the line	Quando vai passando as retas
Of the State of Bahia	Do Estado da Bahia
He says: my God	Ele diz: será meu Deus
Will I come through here again?	Qu'eu passe aqui outro dia?
When the truck enters	Quando o caminhão penetra
Old Minas Gerais State	Na velha Minas Gerais
The poor man, even sadder	O pobre inda vai mais triste
Looking only behind him	Só olhando para traz
The farther the truck goes	Quanto mais o carro anda
The more homesick he becomes.	A saudade aumenta mais.
The truck stops in the middle of the night	Alta noite o carro pára
In the deepest darkness	Na maior escuridão
The poor man goes to lie down	Vai o pobre se deitar
And when he can't sleep on the ground	Quando não dorme no chão
He hangs his hammock from a board	Arma a rede de um pau
On the side of the truck.	Pra grade do caminhão.[75]

---

74 It is no accident that the poet chooses identical language to that of the poet of "Story of Mariquinha e José de Sousa Leão" in describing the road to the South.

75 It is the slats or boards on each side and back of the truck which gives it is name, "parrot cage" ["pau de arara"] and by extension the name to the poor migrants who travel enclosed in it, thus "paus de arara," those who travel in the parrot cage. "Pau de arara" came to be known, and still is today, as the pejorative name of the northeastern migrant in the south of Brazil.

He tries to sleep but can't sleep at all	Vai dormir não dorme nada
Since homesickness grips him tightly	Pois a saudade lhe aperta
He begins to imagine that he goes	Pega imaginar que vai
In search of something uncertain	Atrás duma coisa incerta
Spending the night just thinking	Passa a noite pensativo
On that deserted road.	Naquela estrada deserta.[76]
He hears only the crickets in the caves	Só ouve os grilos nas grutas
Making their chattering sound	Fazendo suas buzinas
And the sad lowing	E os urrados tristonhos
Of the nursing cows nearby	Daquelas vacas turinas
And the fat young yearlings	E dos novilhotes gordos
Owned by the ranchers of Minas Gerais.	Dos fazendeiros de Minas.
When the next day comes	Quando é no outro dia
And the truck moves ahead again	O carro sai novamente
The poor man up there on top	E o pobre vai em cima
Very tired and sick	Muito enfadado e doente
Unable even to move even a little	Sem poder nem se jogar
To the side or forward.	Nem de lado nem de frente.
After nine or ten days go by	Quando faz nove ou dez dias
While he is in the middle of that suffering	Quando vai naquele sofrer
The truck arrives in Rio	O carro chega no Rio
And the poor man tries to climb down	O pobre trata em se descer
But he's so stoved up	Porém vai tão entrevado
That he's scarcely able to move.	Que não pode se mexer.

---

[76] Coincidence or not, the language in this strophe is amazingly similar to the lyrics of Chico Buarque's "Peter the Laborer," here "Pete the Thinker" ["Pedro Penseiro"], a masterpiece of melody and lyric which treats the same theme. The migrant's pondering of an uncertain future, always thinking, always thinking, is certainly a happy coincidence.

In the Plaza of St. Christopher's	No campo de São Cristóvão[77]
The poor man climbs down from the truck	O pobre desce do carro
And walks down the nearest street	E segue de rua afora
Without even a cigarette in his pocket	Sem ter no bolso um cigarro
With the suitcase in his hand	Com a maleta na mão
And his clothes the color of clay.	E a roupa da cor de barro.
And he walks very mistrustfully	E segue desconfiado
Like a wounded bird that can't fly	Como um pássaro que não voa
And he walks on trying to see	E sai olhando para ver
If he can spot anybody	Se avista uma pessoa
From the North that might know him.	Que lhe conheça do Norte
He sees no one, a lost soul.	Não encontra, fica a-toa.[78]
He looks for a job in the construction projects	Pede serviço nas obras
Appealing even to Our Lady	Até por Nossa Senhora
The foreman says:	O encarregado diz:
There are no openings now	Não existe vaga agora
Hey I'm even kicking out	Pois eu já estou botando
The ones in here who have jobs.	Os que têm aqui pra fora.
And thus the poor guy spends	E assim o pobre passa
Three months just hanging around	Três meses no paradeiro
And when he finally gets a job	E quando arranja um serviço
As a bricklayer's helper	De servente de pedreiro
The Institute[79] eats up	O Instituto ainda come
<u>Half of the money</u>.	A metade do dinheiro.

77 The Plaza of São Cristóváó is the location in Rio de Janeiro where several interurban traffic arteries come together, still the main stopping point for truck, bus and car transportation into the north zone of Rio de Janeiro. It appears in the dozens of variations of this poem in the "cordel." As a result, the Sunday morning fair in the same location became the most famous "northeastern" fair in Rio de Janeiro, reaching its apogee from the 1960s to the 1980s. It was said that the fair-goer could experience everything and more that the Northeast had to offer but in Rio de Janeiro -- folk singers, folk poets, poets of "cordel," northeastern food, clothing, hammocks, drink and especially the trademark Northeastern music and dance, the "forró." This writer was a regular at the fair, on and off, for 40 years.

78 The emotive power of this strophe with its wonderful imagery and choice of words is unusual in the "cordel," primarily a narrative poetry. "A-toa" is an amazingly rich adverb in Portuguese; here it captures the absolute loneliness and desolation of the migrant.

79 This refers to the "National Institute of Social Care," ["Instituto de Previdência Social"], similar to Social Security in the United States, a government entity which addresses health matters and retirement for the Brazilian workers. In reality it is far from being able to satisfy the basic social necessities of the masses.

Mark J. Curran

So he works this way for eleven months	Assim trabalha onze meses
Not missing a day or an hour	Sem perder dia e nem hora
But to keep him from completing a year[80]	E para não fazer ano
The boss kicks him out	O patrão bota-o por fora
Giving him a pittance	Lhe dá uma ninharia
Then the poor guy is forced to leave.	Lá o pobre vem embora.
He arrives back up North saying:	Chega no Norte dizendo:
I'll never return to the South	Ao Sul não volto mais
But, poor guy, in one month	Mas coitado, com um mês
He's spent everything and with no job	Gasta tudo e nada faz
He decides to return again	Resolve voltar de novo
He's had it either way.	Fica pra frente e pra traz.
Anyone who has traveled to the South	Quem já viajou pro Sul
Reading this story-poem will embrace me	Lendo este livro me abraça
All this happened to me	Isto passou-se comigo
And it can happen to anyone	E com qualquer um se passa
The thing to do is make the trip	A questão é viajar
And on the day you arrive	Pra no dia que chegar
Tell the same miserable story.[81]	Contar a mesma desgraça.
End	Fim

---

[80] Evidently, in Brazilian labor law, one year's continued work offered certain benefits and stability on the job.

[81] Cícero did indeed live the saga and the odyssey. He is one of the best known of cordelian poets living in Greater Rio (or was until recent years). He ended up a collector [cobrador] on city buses and wrote a poem in the "cordel" telling of the grueling and even dangerous life on the bus lines in Rio.

Cover of one of the story-poems which treat
the poet-singer Ignatius from Catingueira

6.

"Poetic Duel between Patrick and Ignatius from Catingueira"
"Peleja de Patrício e Inácio da Catingueira"
Attributed to Joao Martins de Atayde

This cordelian story-poem is attributed to the poet-publisher Joao Martins de Atayde of Recife, Pernambuco. It is one of the prototypes of the cordelian poems from the oral tradition of the poet-singer-improviser of verse ["cantador"] known as "singer-poet" in this anthology. The singer-poet may also be known as the "Troubadour of the Northeast." The oral poetic duel may take many names in Portuguese – "desafio," "cantoria," "peleja," or "repente," but whatever the nomenclature, this type of poem is the oral poetic duel from Brazil's Northeast between two singers who know how to improvise poetry on the spur of the moment on a given topic or theme. It was originally known as improvised oral verse [poesia repentista], thus presenting a contrast to the traditional written verse appearing in the booklet of cordelian verse. Although there were surely some improvisers of verse from the earliest days of Portuguese colonization in Brazil, the first famous singers date from the last quarter of the 19th century and most hail from the State of Paraíba, the "cradle" of "cordel."

Before seeing the actual poem, it is worthwhile to look at its poetic tradition. The oral poetic duel has its antecedents in Western Tradition in classic Greece in the poetic duels of the shepherds in the works of Theocritus, in the amoeboerum Carmen of the Romans and is registered in Homer, Virgil and Horace. The tradition was passed to Medieval Europe and then to the Renaissance. The tenson or debate from Provence, the "questions and answers" [preguntas y respuestas] of the old Spanish ballad collections and the "verses of love and friends" [trovas de amor e de amigo] from Portugal are just a few of said antecedents. Over time, the tradition was brought to America, the two most notable cases being that of the Argentine poetic counterpoint and duel [" contrapunteo" and "payada"] by the famous "gauchos" of the Argentine plains, and the Brazilian poetic duel.

The poetic duel of the 19th century in the Brazilian Northeast backlands was a true poetic contest between famous singer-poets; today it has evolved into a sort of "rhymed duel" between two poets who are friends and professional colleagues at the same time. The poetic duel of the 19th century, as described by Luís da Câmara Cascudo, the most famous of Brazilian folklorists, was performed with the musical accompaniment of the old "viola," a type of guitar of 9 or 10 metal strings, or on the "rabeca" or "viola de arco," a type of violin used prior to the "rabeca."[82]

The two poets would insult each other, debating in verse using a back and forth "challenge and response," showing off their knowledge of history, mythology or geography, each one "constructing" his poetic, metaphorical "castle" ["marco"]. The lines of verse were filled with exaggeration and braggadocio on the part of each poet.

At times, with the evolution of the poetic duel, some poets would use actual memorized verse called "obra feita" in Portuguese, but the good poet could always dominate an opponent by means of rapid and clever improvisation. The poet duel was originally sung in strophes of four lines, [a quadra], with eight syllables to the verse and in the xaxa rhyme scheme. The four-line strophe gradually disappeared in the written form of the duel in the chapbook or pamphlet of cordelian verse and was replaced by the strophe of seven or eight lines of verse.

Often the singer was illiterate, like Ignácio da Catingueira, but others knew how to read and were familiar with the classic books of the Brazilian backlands: the standard almanaque, ["Lunário Perpétuo"] of the times, the "Abbreviated Missal," ["Missal Abreviada"] or basic guide for Catholics at mass, or even the famous "History of the Emperor Charlemagne and the Twelve Knights of France," ["História do Imperador Carlos Magno e dos Doze Pares da França"].[83]

---

82 This author had the pleasure of hearing a blind folk singer sing old ballads accompanying himself on the "rabeca" in Juazeiro do Norte, Ceará, in 1966. Juazeiro is a famous site of religious pilgrimage in the Northeast, the town of Father Cícero, famous priest-healer of the backlands who died in 1934.
83 This information was taken from Luís da Câmara Cascudo's classic "Cowboys and Singers," ["Vaqueiros e Cantadores"], (Porto Alegre: Editora Globo, 1939).

Some of the singers also wrote their own poems to be printed in the booklets of "cordel," but it is generally recognized today that the most famous poetic duels in "cordel" were partially or even totally composed by cordelian poets who "collected" oral verse from the people, or even invented their own "literary" version of the famous oral duels, the written form being directed to a reading public.

Perhaps the most famous poetic duel, an integral part today of Brazil's northeastern folklore, is the "Duel between Romano and Inácio," ["Peleja entre Romano e Inácio"], a duel now made myth in the Northeast. It involved Romano Mãe D'Agua and the same Inácio da Catingueira. According to popular opinion the duel lasted eight days and nights and was a ferocious battle finally won by Romano, a semi-literate poet, who won by using "science" from formal studies to defeat Inácio. Today, few believe the business of the "eight day duel," and in fact, most scholars and even the cordelian poets themselves do not believe there ever was such a duel. What is certain is that there were many variations of the supposed duel transcribed to "cordel" by no less than Leandro Gomes de Barros, Francisco das Chagas Batista and João Martins de Atayde, famous early bards of "cordel." Folklorist Luís da Câmara Cascudo believes that the original version/adaptation was done by one of the most famous singer-poets of the 19th century, Ugolino Nunes da Costa of Paraíba State.

The duel chosen for this anthology is between the same Inácio da Catingueira and José Patrício de Siqueira Patriota, a poet born in Monteiro, Paraíba State. The latter, semi-literate, will duel the famous black slave Inácio, who was born in 1845 and died in 1881, a poet in the inventory of slaves of the epoch who died of a case of pneumonia contracted in the annual burning of the sugar cane fields. According to one scholar, Inácio was a "genius," and no one could overcome the "grace, spontaneity and beauty" of his improvised verse.[84] We choose this duel because of its famous participants and because it contains so many of the classic traits of the old, Northeastern poetic duel -- the braggadocio tone, the traded insults and the racial question of the times.

---

84 See Veríssimo de Melo, <u>Cantador de Viola</u> (Recife: Coleção Concórdia, 1967).

"Poetic Duel of Patrick with
Ignatius from Catingueira"[85]
Attributed to João Martins de Atayde

"Peleja de Patrício com
Inácio da Catingueira"
Atribuído a J. M. de Atayde

P – My name is Joseph Patrick
From Siqueira Patriota
My fists knock out teeth
Blows to knock your head off
The singer who challenges me
Better count on defeat.

P - Me chamo José Patrício
De Siqueira Patriota
Dou tapa que arranca dente
Dou murro que descangota
Cantador que vem a mim
Só pode contar derrota.

I. I was baptized as Ignatius
My nickname, Catingueira
I was raised in Piancó[86]
But I learned to sing in Teixeira[87]
I've slaughtered more than ten thousand
Just while strolling up the hill.

I - Me batizei por Inácio
Por alcunha, Catingueira
Me criei em Piancó
Mas aprendi em Teixeira
Fiz mais de dez mil carniças
Logo ao subir da ladeira.

P- Ignatius, you better sing extra well
'Cause I'm not one to fool around with
I can twist the trunk of a tree
I make firewood out of big trees
God help you if you ever
Dream of going back to Catingueira.

P - Inácio, canta com jeito
Que não sou de brincadeira
Eu torço braúna velha
Faço facho de aroeira
Deus o livre que você
Vá por sonho a Catingueira.

I. Patrick, you are wrong
You should know as a poet
In the backlands where you were
A big tree never grew
God help you if you ever
Dream of going to Catingueira.

I. Patrício, você se engana
Cuidado mais na carreira
No sertão que você foi
Nunca nasceu aroeira
Deus o livre que você
Vá por sonho a Catingueira.

P-Ignatius, here's some advice
Just doing you a favor
My arm weighs a lot
My thinking is rigorous
If you fall into my hands
It will all be over.

P - Inácio, vou te avisar
Fazer-te uma caridade
Meu braço tem muito peso
Meu gênio rigoridade
Se caíres em minhas unhas
Encontras barbaridade.

---

85 "Catingueira" is a small town in the state of Paraíba where this famous black slave singer was born.
86 Piancó is another small town in the interior of Paraíba state.
87 "Teixeira" was the famous region in the interior of Paraíba known as the birthplace of famous singer-poets of the 19th century such as Bernardo Nogueira and the singer-poets of the Nunes da Costa family.

I-Patrick, I'm an old man	I - Patrício, eu já sou passado
An old man has no illusions	E um passado no se ilude
I never found a weight	Eu nunca encontrei um peso
Too big to overcome	Que por grande não me ajude
God willing at the end of the day	Queira Deus no fim da causa
He won't change his mind.	Seu pensamento no mude.
P-Well you seem to think	P - Você parece que entende
That I'm just a toy	Que eu sirvo de brinquedo
I make fun of storms	Eu zombo de tempestade
Night owls don't scare me[88]	Corisco não me faz medo
Prepare for a disaster	Espere pela desgraça
Which is headed your way soon.	Que há de chegar muito cedo.
I – Patrick, just calm down	I - Patrício, se acomode
You are no lion	O senhor não é leão
The lion is of course ferocious	O leão, mesmo é feroz
But one day loses his strength	E um dia perde a ação
A man does him in	Um homem dá cabo nele
Kills him or puts him in a cage.	Mata-o, bota-o, na prisão.
P – I have nothing to do with that	P - Nada tenho a ver com isto
A lion matters little to me	Pouco me importa o leão
When I was born, the midwife	Quando eu nasci, a parteira
Shouted out, "a Samson has been born!."[89]	Gritou: nasceu um Sansão!
They immediately asked my fortune to be told	Mandaram ver minha sina
And they saw the sign of Roland.[90]	Viram os sinais de Roldão.

---

88 The poet uses "owls" in Portuguese in the same context as "black cat" in standard English in the U.S.A..

89 This biblical figure in Northeastern popular culture is a symbol of physical strength and was a victim of Dalila when she cut his hair, thus taking away the source of his great strength. There is a cordelian poem based on the same title from the U.S. cinema.

90 The nephew of Charlemagne, the most famous of the Twelve Knights of France, died combating the rebellious Basques opposed to French dominion of the area. He is known as a figure of super-human courage in Northeastern Brazil, important in the heroic cycle of poems of "cordel."

Mark J. Curran

I – You, sir, seem to hold Samson
As an object or heroic model
A man whose strength
Was all in his hair
Just read the book about Roland[91]
To see how it all unraveled.

P – Samson was of much fame
Roland was king of the warring knights
No one could conquer him
Not even Oliver himself[92]
He [Roland] having the name most feared
Of those legendary warriors.

I – Patrick, for this man
You have much admiration
You seem pretty full of yourself
When you talk about Samson
But for me the most valiant
Was the one who killed Roland.

P – Oh, black man, don't get smart with me
Or I'll really get peeved
And if I really reach the limit
A piece of a star will fall on you
I'll make a suitcase of your skin
And bed slats of your bones.

I – And I plan to make
From your hide a large belt
From your legs, two clubs
From your arms, butter whips
From your head, a fry pan
And from your neck, a tall bottle.

I - Vossa mercê tem Sansão
Como objeto ou modelo
Um homem que a sua força
Estava toda no cabelo
Leia o livro de Roldão
Veja agora o desmantelo.

P - Sansão teve muita fama
Roldão foi rei dos guerreiros
Não pôde exceder com êle
Nem o próprio Oliveiros
Sendo o nome mais temido
Dos lutadores primeiros.

I - Patrício tem este homem
Com uma admiração
Parece que fica amplo
Quando se fala em Sansão
Para mim o mais valente
Foi o que matou Roldão.

P - Oh! Negro, não me repliques
Se não com pouco me agasto
E se eu sair dos limites
Cai um pedaço de astro
Faço do teu couro mala
Dos ossos, cama de lastro.

I - E eu pretendo fazer
Do seu couro um cinturão
Das canelas, dois cacetes
Dos braços, mão de pilão
Da cabeça, uma panela
E do pescoço, um botijão.

---

91 Among the many romances on the theme in Brazil, perhaps the most famous, referred to here, was "The Death of the Twelve Knights of France," ["A Morte dos Doze Pares da França"]. The entire cycle of cordelian poems is based on the book "Story of the Emperor Charlemagne and the Twelve Knights of France" ["História do Imperador Carlos Magno e dos Doze Pares de França"] Lisbon, circa 1863.

92 Oliver ["Oliveiros"] was another of the knights of Charlemagne; in the popular ballads he battles the fierce Turkish warrior, "Ferrabrás," King of Alexandria, son of the great Admiral Balán.

P – Ignatius, have you forgotten
What Romano already did to you?[93]
Well I'm now going to prove to you
That I'm even more of a tyrant.
I'll leave you blind for six months
And crippled for more than a year.

I – Mr. Romano did nothing to me
In fact he was afraid of me
But he used writing
In order to put an end to me
He was so afraid he turned
White the color of marble.

P – Ignatius, just open your eyes
I had already planned
Before leaving this place
To make a stew out of you
And I never made a plan
That didn't turn out well.

I - I invited three people
To swallow up a mixed-blood
One of them was Hugolino[94]
Who is a master in my trade
And he already invited a lot of folks
To have Patrick for lunch.

P – Just the same my enemy
My flesh he does not buy
If you dare to go there
You'll meet one hell of a mulatto
My skin is like solid steel
No bullet can go through it.

P - Inácio, estás esquecido
Do que já te fez Romano
Pois eu agora te provo
Que agora sou mais tirano
Te deixo cego 6 meses
E aleijado mais de um ano.

I - Sr. Romano nada fez-me
Pois teve medo de mim
Valeu-se da escritura
Para poder dar-me fim
Teve medo que ficou
Branco da cor de marfim.

P - Inácio, abre teu olho
Que eu já tinha projetado
Antes de sair daqui
Fazer de ti um guizado
E nunca fiz um cálculo
Que não visse o resultado.

I - Eu convidei três pessoas
Para comer um mestiço
Um deles foi Hugolino
Que é mestre em meu oficio
Já convidou muita gente
Para almoçar do Patrício.

P - Ainda o meu inimigo
De minha carne não compra
Se você meter-se nisto
Encontra um mulato estrompa
Meu couro é dum aço seco
Não há metralha que rompa.

---

93 A reference to the already mentioned famous duel between Ignatius and Romano (that of the 8 days and nights) and Ignatius' loss to the latter.
94 Another poet-singer of the Nunes da Costa family near Teixeira, Paraíba state, a figure made myth for his prodigious memory. According to local folklore, he memorized the entire "Bible" as well as other popular books of the era.

I – For me it will turn soft
Soft just like glue
There's no steel, however strong
That rust can't eat it up
Even if you lean on
The Holy Father in Rome.[95]

P – Ignatius, you were a slave
And you had no education
That's common with all slaves
They never have good upbringing
They just want to take liberties
With their owner or their boss.

I – Patrick, sure I was a slave
But I was held in good esteem
And I had a lady
Who walked hand in hand with me
Weren't you born free?
Just where is your good upbringing?

P - My father was a poor man
He could not send me to school
But I learned to read
And to count perfectly
There's no trace of black blood in me
You can tell when I talk.

I - Well your skin is black
And your hair is mighty kinky
Your teeth are large and white
And your gums quite red
In color, we're just the same
You look almost like me.

P - I am dark, I'll admit
And my hair is kinky
But no man in this world
Put out a penny for me
Not like you and your grandparents
Who were sold on the slave block.

I - Para mim torna-se mole
Macio como uma goma
Não há aço por ser forte
Que ferrugem não o coma
Ainda que você se valha
Do padre santo de Roma.

P - Inácio tu foste escravo
Não tivera educação
Sempre o comúm do escravo
É nunca ter criação
Pois quer tomar liberdade
Com o senhor ou patrão.

I - Patrício, eu fui escravo
Porém tive estimação
Uma senhora que tive
Andou comigo na mão
O senhor não nasceu livre?
Quedê sua educaço?

P - Meu pai era homem pobre
Não podia me educar
Mas aprendi a ler
E perfeitamente contar
Não tenho traço de negro
Se vê logo onde eu falar.

I - Como tens o couro preto
E o cabelo pixaim
Os dentes alvos e largos
As gengivas roxas assim
Nas cores somos iguais
Estás muito perto de mim.

P - Sou moreno, reconheço
Meu cabelo é pixaim
Porém, homem neste mundo
Não deu dinheiro por mim
Não és tu, que tens avós
Vendidos tiveram fim.

---

95 The pope, of course.

I – Patrick, this obliges me To end my patience Hearing someone call "dark" The color of toasted coffee Your grandfather came to Brazil Just to be put on the block.	I - Patrício, esta me obriga A ficar muito agastado Em ouvir chamar moreno A cor de café torrado Seu avô veio ao Brasil Para ser negociado.
P – Ignatius, I know that you know All about all our ancestors Let's just talk about things of today Let's forget about the backward days Let's end the discussion We both need to rest.	P - Ignácio, sei que conheces Os nossos antepassados Tratemos só da moderna Esqueçamos os atrasados Acabemos com discussão Ficaremos descansados.
I-Well, this is another matter I don't battle without a motive You sir also need to forget about The people that were captives He who lives in a glass house Does not throw stones.	I - Isto assim é outra coisa Eu não luto sem motivo Vossa mercê também esqueça O povo que foi cativo Quem tem defunto ladrão Não fala em roubo de vivo.
End, Juazeiro do Norte, Ceará, printing of January 4, 1965	FIM, Juazeiro, tiragem de 4-1-65

Cover of the story-poem "The Encounter of Tancredo with St. Peter in Heaven" by Chiquinho do Pandeiro and Master Azulão

7.

"The Encounter of Tancredo with St. Peter in Heaven"
"O Encontro de Tancredo com São Pedro no Céu"
Chiquinho do Pandeiro and Master Azulão

This story-poem deals with politics and the economic situation of Brazil in the late 1980s. It follows a long tradition of the story-poems as reporting and a type of folk-popular journalism – accounts in narrative poems dealing with the most important political, economic and historic events which take place within the Brazilian reality. The theme of politics is important and loved by the cordelian public and the poet of "cordel." Among other functions that the latter exercises in his humble milieu, is that of a true reporter and interpreter of the events that most affect his public. This tradition comes from the very beginnings of "cordel," since among the first verses extant are those that treat the War of Canudos in 1896-1897 and its destruction by federal troops, including the death of the messianic figure "Anthony the Counselor, ["Antônio Conseleiro"].

The story of the social-political-religious odyssey of Father Cícero Romão Batista of tiny Juazeiro do Norte, Ceará, from the 1880s to the 1930s followed a few years after the War of Canudos. Father Cícero became the most heralded religious figure of all "cordel" and one of its great heroes. In the first three decades of the twentieth century "cordel" also documented the entire saga of the northeastern bandits, revealing in verse facts and fantasy of real-life bandits [cangaceiros] Antônio Silvino, Lampião and his consort Maria Bonita. The death of the latter two took place in a bloody ambush at the Angicos Ranch in the State of Sergipe in 1938, a scene not dissimilar to the finale of "Bonny and Clyde" in the U.S. Cinema.

"Cordel" indeed chronicled major and minor events of Brazilian life, local and national politics from their beginnings up to the present date. From the Revolutions of Juazeiro in 1914, Rio de Janeiro in 1924, and São Paulo in 1932; the "reign" of Brazil's greatest president, Getúlio

Vargas from 1930 to 1954; the democracy and chaos of nation-builder Juscelino Kubitschek of Brasilia fame; the president-college professor Janio Quadros of São Paulo; the turn to the left of João "Jango" Goulart in the early 1960s; the Peasants' Movement of the 1960s and their flirtation with Fidel Castro's Cuba; the military coup-revolution and "Pax Militar" of the succeeding dictatorships from 1964 to 1985; the return to democracy with the great victory and subsequent tragic death of democratic hero Tancredo Neves; and the ups and downs, scandals and reforms of presidents since then. "Cordel" documents most recently the regime of the northeastern-born national labor leader Luís Inácio da Silva, or "Lula" as they call him in Brazil.[96]

All the great poets of "cordel" in Brazil – Leandro Gomes de Barros, Francisco das Chagas Batista, João Melquíades Ferreira da Silva, João Ferreira de Lima, João Martins de Atayde, Rodolfo Coelho Cavalcante – and many more than can be mentioned here, wrote poems of history and politics, and the vision that they presented is a true popular documentation of the national political reality from the point of view and in the language of the masses.

João José dos Santos, pseudonym Azulão, a Paraíban poet living for many years in greater Rio de Janeiro (he actually lived for years in a poor suburb called Engenheiro Pedreira) is perhaps the most talented of the poets of recent years who write on politics. Azulão is first of all a good poet; he handles popular imagery, metrics, rhyme and language exceptionally well. But he is passionate about politics.[97] Azulão writes in a satiric and humorous style, using a piquant, biting black humor, of

[96] We dedicated many years to the study and writing of this phenomenon of "cordel" as journalism and popular history in Brazil, culminating in the book "History of Brazil in 'Cordel'" [História do Brasil] em Cordel.(São Paulo: Editora da Universidade de São Paulo, 1998, 2nd. ed. 2001).

[97] Azulão (João José dos Santos) was a candidate for town council in Engenheiro Pedreira some years back. One of the tools of his electoral campaign was his story-poems of "cordel; he used the back covers as advertising and propagandizing for his campaign. He won the election, but the election was declared null because advertising used his pen name or pseudonym on the booklets of "cordel" rather than his given, baptismal name as registered in the municipality, a process repeated as well as on the actual ballot. The poet was naturally infuriated and battled the injustice of the case for years. As a result he became understandably bitter about the political system.

the events that most affect Brazil. The poem chosen for this chapter in the anthology, like many others by Azulão, comments on the political and social reality of the Brazil of the late 1980s. In this poem Azulão declares dual authorship with one Chico do Pandeiro, but the poem undeniably reflects the former's traditional style and manner.

Aside from commenting on the death of Tancredo Neves, the great democrat and political messiah who was instrumental in bringing about the freedom of Brazilians accustomed to a military regime of twenty-one years, he writes of Neves' successor, the writer-intellectual-politician José Sarney and the terrible dilemma that this president confronted in a country that many called "ungovernable." Azulão touches upon economics, the privileges of the governing, terrible corruption, and his favorite theme – those politicians who sold the best of Brazil to the interests of international capitalism.

The story-poem uses a topic or technique familiar to old "cordel:" the message sent by a beloved political leader, now deceased, from heaven to those on earth. Almost all the great politicians, from Getúlio Vargas to Juscelino Kubitschek and even General Castelo Branco (the first military president during the long dictatorship from 1964-1985), speak with their public in letters that appear in the cordelian literature. The passing of past political greats is an ever present phenomenon in the panorama of "cordel," whether treating the traumatic goodbye and suicide of Getúlio Vargas, the car wreck which took Juscelino Kubitschek who founded and built Brasília, or even the most recent tragedy of Brazil: the sickness, the seven surgeries and the slow death of the "political messiah" Tancredo Neves who freed Brazil from the hands of the military. The tradition of the use of heaven and hell in "cordel" is old: the good leaders went to heaven where they had their debates with St. Peter and Jesus Christ himself, while the evil ones, Hitler and Mussolini being the most famous, were sent to cordelian hell where they jousted with Satan or flirted with his daughter or wife, or even tried to take over from Satan. The tradition now continues in a modern and critical discourse which documents the age.

Mark J. Curran

| "The Encounter of Tancredo with St. Peter in Heaven" | "O Encontro de Tancredo com São Pedro no Céu" |
| Chiquinho do Pandeiro and Master Azulão | C. do Pandeiro e Mestre Azulão |

Oh holy and divine muse
Cover me with your veil
So that I may write a poem
Which will serve as a trophy
The encounter of Tancredo[98]
With St. Peter up there in heaven.

Tancredo Neves battled
For a progressive Brazil to go forward
He defeated Paulo Maluf[99]
Becoming our president
With him the people expected
A very different Brazil.

On the eve of assuming power
Tancredo became ill
He was quickly hospitalized
But the doctors had no solution
He had eight operations
There was no quick fix; he died.

Tancredo rose up to heaven
Rising with thousands looking on
He was very impressed
Seeing the sky a bright blue[100]
St. Peter praised him
For having left Brazil!

Oh musa santa divina
Me cobra com vosso véu
Pra mim escrever um livro
Que servirá de troféu
O encontro de Tancredo
Com São Pedro lá no céu.

Tancredo Neves lutou
Para o Brasil ir a frente
Ganhou de Paulo Maluf
Pra ser nosso Presidente
Com ele o povo esperava
Um Brasil bem diferente.

Na véspera de assumir
O Tancredo adoeceu
E foi internado as pressas
Médico nem um jeito deu
Sofreu oito operações
Não houve jeito, morreu.

Tancredo subiu ao céu
Voando com mais de mil
Ficou muito admirado
Em ver o céu cor de anil
São Pedro lhe elogiou
Por ter deixado o Brasil!

---

98 The hero of the story-poem is Tancredo Neves, politician from Minas Gerais State and president-elect of Brazil in January of 1985 after a tremendously hard fought populist campaign for "direct elections now" [the military had not allowed direct presidential elections for years]. Neves became known as the author of the "New Republic," that is, the first Brazilian democratic government since the military revolution of 1964.

99 Ex-mayor of the huge city of São Paulo, the "locomotive" of Brazil, governor of the same state, the most powerful and rich in the Republic, Paulo Maluf was a wealthy conservative and candidate of the P.D.S. party in the campaign of 1984 against Tancredo Neves and his running mate José Sarney. Tancredo won, thus ending almost twenty-one years of military government in Brazil.

100 The "blue" the poet chooses happens to be the same "blue" on the Brazilian national flag.

St. Peter said: Tancredo,
All heaven is very happy
Because you sir now
Belong to our country
You are better off here
Than being President there.

Besides that, you have
A very good heart
You couldn't stay there
Where there is only corruption
And govern a country
Which is chock full of thieves

Tancredo said: Sarney[101]
Is down there all fouled up
With the foreign debt
Strikes on every side
If God does not help him
He's flat out screwed.

There are strikes everywhere
In the ports, the hospitals,
It's either the bank workers' strike
Or the subway or the Central Station.[102]
They already tried to set fires
In the Federal District.[103]

São Pedro disse: Tancredo,
O céu está todo contente
Porque o senhor agora
Pertence ao país da gente
Você aqui está melhor
Do que lá ser presidente.

Além disso você tem
Um bondoso coração
Não podia ficar lá
Que só tem corrjupção
E governor um país
Que está assim de ladrão.

Tancredo disse: o Sarney
Lá está todo enrolado
Com dívida no estrangeiro
E greve por todo lado
Se Deus não lhe ajudar
José Sarney está lascado.

Pra todo lado tem greve
No porto, no hospital.
É a greve dos bancários
Metrô e trem da Central.
Já quiseram botar fogo
No Distrito Federal.

---

101 Ex-governor of the northeastern state of Maranhão, later federal senator in Brasília and leader of the P.D.S., Sarney was one of the dissidents of the government party who joined Tancredo Neves' P.M.D.B. and ended being elected as vice-president in January of 1985. With the grave illness and subsequent death of Tancredo, Sarney looked in the mirror and saw himself as the leader of a country which from the very beginning did not like or want him.

102 The "Central Station" refers to the main downtown train station in Rio de Janeiro with the network of trains leaving the city taking the working masses from their jobs in the city to the far suburbs. The Central Station was the subject of the prize winning Brazilian film of recent years past, nominated for "Best Foreign Film" in Hollywood.

103 The Federal District is in the capital city of Brasília.

In Rio Moreira Franco[104]	No Rio Moreira Franco
Came in putting his foot down	Já entrou metendo a sola
Street merchants can sell no more	Camelô não vende mais
Guaraná[105] or Coca-Cola	Guaraná nem Coca-Cola
They are now saying that he	Já estão dizendo que ele
Is worse than Brizola.	Está pior do que o Brizola.
As well the minimum salary	Também o salário mínimo
Turned into confusion	Transformou-se em confusão
When it does come, it's lowered	Quando sai é rebatado
By the fury of inflation	Na fúria da inflação
The thief robs the little man	O ladrão rouba o pequeno
And the powerful rob the thief.	E o grande rouba o ladrão.
Tancredo said: St. Peter,	Tancedo disse: São Pedro,
I, since I did not want to rob,	Eu como não quis roubar
I preferred to leave the earth	Preferi deixar a terra
And come to live in heaven	E vir para o Céu morar
I left José Sarney there	Lá deixei José Sarney
Getting screwed in my place.	Se lascando em meu lugar.
St. Peter said: You sir	São Pedro disse: o Senhor
Is a good citizen	É um cidadão de bem
Down there below things are fouled up	Lá em baixo está sem jeito
Thieves come and go	Ladrão vai e ladrão vem
If you had stayed there	Se você ficasse lá
You would have been a thief too.	Virava ladrão também.
St. Peter said: Tancredo,	São Pedro disse: Tancredo
You are a gentleman	Você é muito gentil
Sit down and calmly	Se sente com toda calma
Tell me in a subtle way	E diga num tom sutil
What's the situation	Qual é a situação
Of politics in Brazil.	Da Política no Brasil.

---

104 He succeeded Leonel Brizola as governor of the State of Rio de Janeiro, but from the masses' point of view there was no bettering of social conditions.

105 Guaraná is a plant from the Amazon region whose seed produces a stimulant used in certain medicines as well as in the national soft-drink of the same name, with local favorites according to one's region of the country.

We here all know	Nós aqui todos sabemos
That things aren't going well there	Que a coisa lá ainda ruim
Please, have no fear,	Você não tenha recelo
Tell it all, detail by detail	Conte tim-tim por tim-tim
Then Tancredo sat down	Aí Tancredo sentou-se
And began, saying the following.	E começou dizendo assim.
Brazil is totally lost	O Brasil está perdido
And there's no one to save it	E não há quem o socorra
Full of whores and queers	Cheio de piranha e viado[106]
It's turned into Sodom and Gomorrah	Virou Sodoma e Gomorra
Young thieves[107] in the middle of the street,	Pivete no meio das ruas
Robbing and shouting, "run."	Roubando e gritando, corra.
Sarney entered into the presidential palace	Sarney entrou no Palácio
Saying: I'll solve everything	Dizendo: tudo eu resolvo
He started the "Cruzado Plan"[108]	Lançou o Plano Cruzado
A new and strong currency	Um dinheiro forte e novo
Later he started a second plan	Depois lançou o Segundo
That was when the masses were screwed.	Aí desgraçou o povo.

---

106 In the Portuguese there is a clever play-on words: "piranha," the voracious flesh-eating fish of Amazon waters, is also the slang in Brazil for "whore." "Viado," meaning the animal "deer" is the common slang for "queer."

107 "Pivete" ["thief"] is the Brazilian word for the young, sometimes vicious urchin-thief so common in recent years. There was a commercial film in Brazil in the 1980s with the same title, "Pivete." Its star, a real delinquent recruited from the streets, was shot down in a slum in Rio a few years after the filming.

108 "The 'Cruzado Plan," [o plano cruzado] of January 28, 1986, was an effort by the Sarney government (under the guidance of the minister of Finance Funaro) to battle against the terrible inflation by reforming the monetary system – something similar to the creation of the "austral" in Argentina during the Alfonsín regime – creating a new currency and establishing the checking of prices by the public itself in supermarkets and shops in urban centers. The government published a list of "fixed" prices of commodities in newspapers throughout the country, and civilians were invited to turn in merchants in shops and super markets who violated the prices. Television news was replete with stories of angry customers, customers of all social class and color, shaking their fingers at the merchants and waving the price lists in front of them. In fact some merchants were hauled before the courts to explain their price gouging. It was a success ... for six months.

With all that, the minimum salary Lost all its value and status The poor man goes to the store He sees meat, but he does not eat any The bloodsucking merchant[109] only plans To starve the poor man of hunger.	Com isso o salário mínimo Perdeu o valor e nome O pobre vai pro mercado Vê carne, porém não come Que o tubarão só pretende Matar o povo de fome.
Sarney froze the prices Thus squeezing the sharks He who disobeyed the law Would go directly to prison And the customer himself Would do all the checking it out.[110]	Sarney congelou os preços Apertando o tubarão Quem desrespeitou a lei Ia direto a prisão E o próprio freguês fazia Sua fiscalização.
As a result of that noble attitude The masses were content They believed in the "cruzado" And in the plan of the president But the good news only lasted Some nine months.	Com essa nobre atitude O povo ficou contente Acreditou no cruzado E o plano do Presidente Mas esse bom só durou Uns nove meses somente.
The "movers" against Sarney Created all kinds of pressure They withheld meat and milk Sugar, butter and bread That was when Sarney turned over Brazil to the sharks.	Os grandes contra o Sarney Fizeram toda pressão Esconderam carne e leite Açúcar, manteiga e pão Aí Sarney entregou O Brasil pro tubarão.
Today on the backs of the masses It's the shark that's mounted up Prices are up one thousand per cent The whole nation is dizzy And the reins of Brazil Are in the hands of the sharks.	Hoje nas costas do povo O tubarão é quem monta Já aumentou mil por cento A nação toda está tonta E as rédeas do Brasil O tubarão tomou conta.
Ranchers suck the blood Of the people, like leeches Denying milk to the children In day care and in orphanages Preferring to throw it into the rivers Rather than selling it cheaper.	Pecuarista suga o sangue Do povo igual carrapato Nega o leite das crianças De crèche e de orfanato Prefere jogar nos rios Do que vender mais barato.

---

109 There is an expression in Brazil, "o tubarão do comércio," [the business shark], that is, the owner of a shop, a market, a supermarket, who charges high prices to get rich at the expense of the poor.

110 See note 13.

Now because the owner of the cattle	Porque o dono do gado
Is a senator, or a mayor	É senador, é prefeito
Who treat the laws of the country	Que ferem as leis do país
With the greatest disrespect	Com o maior desrespeito
The government knows about it all	O governo sabe tudo
But can't solve the problem.	Porém não pode dar jeito.
It's like the old saying	É como o velho ditado
My grandmother used to say	Que dizia a minha avó
"Happiness for the poor man	"Que alegria do pobre
Lasts just one day"	É durante um dia só
Perhaps being a kilo of tripe	Por ser um quilo de tripa
Viscerals and pig's knuckles.	Um bofe e um mocotó.
In the Ministry in Brasília	No Ministério em Brasília
Reigns confusion all day long	Tem confusão toda hora
Minister Saad resigned[111]	Saad renunciou
Funaro already had split the scene	Funaro já caiu fora
Being a thief, he's got a job	Sendo ladrão tem emprego
Being honest, he's got to leave.	Sendo justo vai embora.
The government's party	O partido do governo
Is almost demolished	Está quase demolido
The fact is the Cruzado n. 2	Que o segundo cruzado
Messed up the party's plans	Bagunçou com o partido
The people quit believing	O povo perdeu a crença
And the government's bankrupt.	E o governo está falido.
There are some new thieves now	Tem agora uns ladrões novos
They're called "maharajas"	Chamados de marajais
Robbing worse than rats	Roubando que só uns ratos
The ones in the sugar cane fields	Desses de canaviais
And in the state governments	Dos governos dos estados
Each one robs even more.	Cada um que rouba mais.

---

[111] João Sayad was Minister of Planning at the beginning of the Sarney regime. He opposed the monetary plan of the first Minister of Finance in the Sarney regime, Dornelles, who later resigned. Then Dilson Funaro came in, one of the creators of the "Cruzado" Plan. With the failure of the "Cruzado Plan II," Sayad continued the battle, this time against Funaro. Everything ended in March of 1987 with Sayad's resignation .

The guy who wants to be president now	Quem quer ser o presidente
Is that guy Brizola[112]	De lá agora é o Brizola
So he too can get his hand in	Pra também meter a mão
Until he fills up his bag	Até encher a sacola
Creating confusion all over again	Criar outra confusão
And leaving Brazil begging.	E deixar o Brasil de esmola.
Figueiredo[113] enlarged even more	Figueiredo aumentou mais
Our debt to America	Nossa dívida americana
Sending Delfim[114] to get	Mandando Delfim buscar
More money every week	Dinheiro toda semana
And by the end of the mandate	E no final do mandato
They had divided the "dough."	Eles dividiram a grana.
They have in Swiss banks	Têm nos bancos de Suiça
True piles of money	Verdadeiros cabedais.
All at the cost to Brazil	Tudo às custas do Brasil
And we with our minerals	Com os nossos minerais
And beyond that, they are partners	Além de tudo são sócios
In the multinationals.	Das multinacionais.
Delfim has so much money	Delfim tem tanto dinheiro
That he's swollen with fat	Que de gordo está inchado
The people in São Paulo	O povo de São Paulo
Are so dumb and brazen	É tão burro e descarado
That they still elected Delfim	Que ainda elegeu Delfim
To be their federal congressman.	Para ser seu deputado.

---

112 Leonel Brizola, the veteran politician from Rio Grande do Sul State, once following the line of Getúlio Vargas, was exiled by the military for his leftist tendencies, but after the amnesty of the later years of the military regime, he is back with more vigor than ever, getting himself elected to the governorship of Rio de Janeiro State, and now in the running for president of the country.

113 Figueiredo was the last military president (João Figueiredo, 1979-1985) who really favored the gradual political opening, but in spite of it offered his own candidate for the presidency.

114 Antônio Delfim Neto was Minister of Finance during the so-called "boom" or "Brazilian economic miracle" from 1968-1974. He returned to the same post in August of 1979 when Simonson resigned. Delfim always was in favor of economic growth at any cost (financed by more foreign capital through new loans). The irony is that while the poor Brazilian's belt was stretched ever tighter by the failing economy, Delfim grew fatter!

Every little bit of Amazonia	A Amazônia todinha
Is now in American hands	Já é Americana
They have rockets and atomic bombs	Têm foguete e bomba atômica
Enough arms to fight for a year	Armas para brigar um ano
If Brazil does something stupid	Se o Brasil meter-se à besta
It will just go down the tubes.	Só vai entrar pelo cano.
The Americans have arms	O americano tem armas
So sophisticated and powerful	Sofisticada e possante
That if Brazil wants to fight	So Brasil quiser brigar
It's all over in a minute	Se arrasa num instante
Same thing as a small goat	É mesmo que um cabrito
Facing an elephant.	Enfrentar um elefante.
Of all the politicians there's not one	Dos politicos não tem um
Who is a true patriot	Patriota verdadeiro
There are only thieves and the corrupt	Só tem ladrão e corrupto
Who sell out for the dough	Que se vende por dinheiro
That's why they've already sold	Por isso é que já venderam
Brazil to the foreigners.	O Brasil pro estrangeiro.
St. Peter said: it's true	São Pedro disse: é verdade
Brazil is in really bad shape	O Brasil está muito ruim
With the stench of thieves	Empestado de ladrões
And if it continues this way	Se continua assim
Ambition will get to the point	A ambição chega num ponto
They'll end up doing themselves in.	Que eles por si se dão fim.
My view is for them to die	Meu voto é que eles morram
Like fish in the net[115]	Como peixe no jiqui
Jesus already told me: Peter,	Jesus já me disse: Pedro
Keep your eye on them down there	Fique só de olho aí
And don't let even one of those cuckholds	Pra não deixar nem um corno
Ever get in here.	Daqueles entrar aqui.
Jesus is so upset	Jesus está tão revoltado
That he refuses to even talk about them	Que nem sequer fala neles
Satan just ordered someone to tell us	Satanás mandou dizer
That he will take care of them	Que vai tomar conta deles
That over there in the old hell	Que lá no inferno velho
There's a place for all of them.	Tem lugar pra todos eles.

---

115 "Jiqui" is actually a type of basket that is thrown into the water to trap the fish.

So the thief earns his hell
The just is the one who inherits heaven
Dutra, Jango, Juscelino
Getúlio e Carlos Lacerda[116]
They are doing well here and don't want
To talk any more about that shit.

Tancredo said: here I
Am free of all the brouhaha
Of that Brazil always fighting
Brazil of the rats and vultures
I want all of them
To die from drinking rum.

St. Peter said: Tancredo
Take a little advice
Stay here with us folks
Heaven is yours as well
You died for the world
But for God you were just born.

End

O ladrão ganha o inferno
O céu o justo é quem herda
Dutra, Jango, Juscelino
Getúlio e Carlos Lacerda
Aqui estão bem que nem querem
Falar mais naquela merda.

Tancredo disse: eu aqui
Estou livre do sururú
Daquele Brasil de briga
De rato e de urubu
Eu quero é que eles todos
Morram tomando pitú.[117]

São Pedro disse: Tancredo
Tome um conselho meu
Ficar aqui com a gente
Que o céu também é seu
Você morreu para o mundo
Mas pra Deus você nasceu.

Fim

---

[116] All are former presidents except for Carlos Lacerda, ex-governor and opposed to the dictatorship of Getúlio Vargas and later on to "the communist leftist threat" of 1963 and President João Goulart. They were all taken by "cordel" to heaven where they had pleasant conversations with St. Peter or even Jesus Christ, something expected for the social and political heroes of the "literatura de cordel."

[117] "Pitú" is a brand name for a popular northeastern sugar cane rum [cachaça].

Back cover of the story-poem "The End of the War and the Death of Hitler and Mussolini" by Delarme Monteiro da Silva

8.

"The End of the War and the Death of Hitler and Mussolini"
"O Fim da Guerra e a Morte de HITLER e MUSSOLINE"
Delarme Monteiro da Silva

Just as the poet of "cordel" has seen himself as a "poet-reporter" of major local, regional and national events, the same poets also have reported since the beginnings of "cordel" on major international events or personages when these affect the lives and times of Brazilians. Most poets have written at least a minimum amount of story-poems on the topic, although a few totally ignore both the "role" and topic of the "reporter" in "cordel." On the other hand, over the one hundred years existence of this popular literature in verse, there is a significant list of poets who consistently wrote journalistic stories, and a few who excelled in them.

Once again Leandro Gomes de Barros and his contemporary Francisco das Chagas Batista first come to mind. The latter chronicled local and national political events in the early 20th century, but also wrote several important poems on World War I. But it was Leandro who really chronicled in verse the major happenings of his time – the internal politics, the social situation with the droughts and migration, the English presence in the Northeast, and World War I and how it affected internal society in the Northeast.

It was World War I and its aftermath that really brought the United States to the world stage and hence to the attention of the bards of "cordel." The saga of Sacco and Vanzetti and their plight as immigrants in the United States, and the kidnapping of the "prince" of American "aristocracy" -- the son of the Lindberghs -- were just two cases in point. But it was the advent of the American Cinema and its instantly recognized stars that brought an interesting new chapter of America's presence in "cordel:" the use of the photos of stars such as Mickey Rooney, Clark Gable, Gene Autry, Maureen O'Sullivan, Spencer Tracy and others as illustrations on the covers of "cordel."

The conflagration of World War II with its real life villains of the Axis – Hitler, Mussolini and Hirohito – and its heroes – Churchill, Roosevelt and even Stalin at the time – opened a brand new chapter of cordelian reporting on the "world out there." The trend continues to the present: the war in Egypt over the Suez Canal, the Korean War, the Cold War confrontations between the United States and the Soviet Union, and most recently the ideological and real battles for the Middle East. Israel's war with Egypt in 1967, continued conflict with the Palestinians, and the arrival of Osama Bin Laden and Moslem extremist terrorism changed the focus. 9-11, the two wars in Iraq and the "debate between Bush and Bin Laden" continue the trends. There is no reason to expect any change or lack of interest on the part of contemporary poets who succeed in getting their stories in print through the PC and printer at its side or in a "new" cordel on the internet.

We choose a poem at an important time by an excellent poet to exemplify "There's a big world out there:" Delarme Monteiro's "The End of the War and the Death of Hitler and Mussolini," Recife, 1945. Delarme worked as typesetter and general "handy-man" in the stable of poets employed by João Martins de Atayde in Recife during the heyday of "cordel" from the 1930s through the late 1950s. Atayde, a good poet but also enterprising publisher, opened the door to poetic prosperity in 1921 when he purchased the originals of the now deceased (in 1918) Leandro Gomes de Barros from his widow. With the considerable collection of his own poems and those of people like Delarme Monteiro, and now Leandro's, Ataíde was able to mount the most successful "cordel" operation in the Northeast. He continued and expanded upon Leandro's sales network to the point that the "generic" name of cordelian poetry in the late 1940s came to be the "arrecife" or "poem from Recife." This poem by Delarme Monteiro is just one of many true successes of the times.

"The End of the War and the Death
of HITLER AND MUSSOLINI"
Delarme Monteiro

"O Fim da Guerra e a Morte
de HITLER E MUSSOLINE"
Delarme Monteiro

The black shroud was torn That covered the entire world, Saving millions of souls From the bars of captivity From Moscow, Paris, Washington, London and Rio de Janeiro.	Rasgou-se a negra mortalha Que envolvia o mundo inteiro, Salvando milhões de almas Dos grilhões do cativeiro De Moscou, París, Washington, Londres e Rio de Janeiro.
Unhappy is he who wants[118] To be first without any second Without remembering that there exists Another profound power Like the tyrant who insisted On enslaving the world.	Infeliz de quem quer ser Um primeiro sem segundo, Sem se lembrar que existe Um outro poder profundo Como o tirano que quiz Escravizar todo mundo.
That tyrant was Hitler An oppressor of humanity Nephew of tyranny Product of evil, Engenderer of homicide, Son of barbarity.	Esse tirano era Hitler Opressor da Humanidade Sobrinho da tirania Entiado da maldade, Genitor do Homicídio, Filho da Barbaridade.
The Devil crouched In front of the divine power, And the monster hatefully saw What would be his destiny He was killed in his lair, The most uncivilized assassin.	A Besta-fera acuou-se Em frente ao poder divino, E o monstro viu com ódio Qual seria o seu destino Foi morto na sua toca, O mais inculto assassino.

---

118 These first two strophes are indicative of the traditional style employed by this ever-so-traditional cordelian poet in this entire story-poem. The dramatic opening in the first strophe is followed by the traditional moral message in verse setting the tone for the poem. The capital sin of all "cordel" is that of the fallen Lucfer – wanting to be greater than God himself – displaying an undying arrogance in the process. Hitler is just one more example of this in the cordelian poetry.

Mark J. Curran

With the death of this monster	Com a morte deste monstro
People sang "Hosana"	O povo cantou hozana,
The world shouted deliriously	Gritava o mundo em delírio
"Down with the profane beast,"	Abaixo a besta profana
While others shouted,	Emquanto outros gritavam,
"The beast-tyrant was killed."	Foi morta a féra tirana.
This shouting out echoed	Este brado retumbava
Throughout the corners of the earth	Em todos rincões da terra,
Through valleys, rivers and mountains	Por vales rios e montes
To the top of the mountain ranges	Até no topo da serra
As if announcing	Como que prenunciando,
The end of the War to all.	P'ra todos o fim da Guerra.
Within nine days after	Com nove dias depois
The death of the devil-beast,	Da morte da besta féra,
Throughout the entire universe	Para todo o universo
A new era came forth	Despontava nova era
There surged forth on the horizon	Surgia no horizonte,
A new sun of springtime.	Novo sol da Primavera.
The hostilities are over!	Findou-se as hostilidades!
That was the harmonious shout,	Foi o grito harmonioso,
That echoed throughout the world	Que ecoou pelo mundo
Powerful and dizzying	Possante, e vertiginoso
Was the sound of the trumpet	Foi o toque da tombeta,
Of our powerful God.	Do Nosso Deus poderoso.
More than three years ago	Mais a trez anos atraz
It's almost not good to speak of it,	Quase nem é bom falar,
Mourning, suffering and pain	Luto, sofrimento e dores
Were seen everywhere	Se via em todo lugar
Death stalked the world	A morte rondava o mundo,
Never being satiated.	Sem nunca se saciar.
Hitler was at that time	Hitler era nesse tempo
The hangman of the universe	O verdugo do universe
At that time had not turned over	Inda não tinha virado
The coin to the other side	A medalha pelo inverso
All parts of the world obeyed	Todo o mundo obedecia,
His perverse instinct.	Ao seu instinto perverso.

After almost having conquered The peoples of the West He threw all his troops And his infernal tanks From the heavens and on the people Of the eastern lands.	Quaze após ter conquistador Os povos ocidentais, Jogou todas suas tropas E seus tanques infernais Sobre o céu e sobre o povo, Das terras orientais.
Then on one fatal day As head of the Nazis, He said: German people Show your patriotism By invading the great Russia, Capital of Bolshevism.	Então num dia fatal Como chefe do nazismo, Diz ele: povo Alemão Mostrai teu patriotismo Invadindo a grande Rússia, Capital do Bolchivismo.
Defeating this granary We shall have a good food supply And we will take from that land Special armaments To rain down on the Allies, The most violent blows.	Conquistando este celeiro Teremos bons alimentos E tiramos dessa terra Especiais armamentos P'ra vibrar nos aliados, Os golpes mais violentos.
Russia was then invaded And with great ease, Ukraine was occupied And other lands in great number Yet Hitler never dreamed That black destiny was coming.	Foi logo invadida a Rússia Com grande facilidade, Foi ocupada a Ucrânia E terras em quantidade Porém Hitler nem sonhava, Que vinha a fatalidade.
It was then that they united, Russians, English, Americans, Brazilians and Frenchmen And even Italians United in one sole force To combat the tyrant.	Foi então que se ligaram, Russo, Inglêz, Americano, Brazileiros e Francezes Até mesmo Italiano Unidos numa só força P'ra combater o tirano.
Tanks, airplanes and bombs Were sent by the Allies, The Russians were very satisfied And happily accepted them And against the Nazi beast, They marched with much gusto.	Tanques, aviões e bombas Os aliados mandaram, Os russos mui satisfeitos Com alegria aceitaram E contra a féra Nazista, Com muito gusto marcharam.

Mark J. Curran

At this point the Germans Attacked Stalingrad And in this heroic city Stalin well prepared Left Hitler the devil-beast Totally defeated.	Neste ponto os Alemães Atacaram Stalingrado E nesta heróica cidade Stalin bem preparado Deixou Hitler a besta féra, Totalmente derrotado.
From this date commenced The ruination of Germany He no longer had the advantage Nor could Hitler tell big stories The Allies became The commanders of that campaign.	Desta data começou A ruína da Alemanha Não se via mais vantagens Nem Hitler conta façanha Os Aliados ficaram, Senhores da tal campanha.
In the East it was the Russians In the West the Allies, They were surrounding the Nazis With desperate blows, Leaving the Nazi monsters, Smashed under their feet.	No oriente era os russos No ocidente os aliados, Foram cercando o Nazismo Com golpes desesperados Deixando os monstros nazista, Sob seus pés esmagados.
They reconquered Abyssinia France, Italy, in effect, everywhere Poland, Greece, Normandy All were liberated in this way That was when, then, they prepared The invasion of Berlin.	Reconquistaram Abissínia França, Itália, tudo enfim Polonia, Grecia, Normandia Foram libertas assim Foi quando então prepararam, A invasão de Berlim.
Before that, the Allies When they had invaded Italy They searched out Mussolini Preparing his burial shroud But he fled to the north In order not to end the battle.	Antes disso, os aliados Quando invadiram a Italia Procuraram Mussoline P'ra cortar sua mortalha Este fugiu para o norte P'ra não pôr fim à batalha.
Mussolini was the friend Of the Nazi devil-beast He also considered himself a god This fascist clown But this one the Allies Already had put on the list.	Mussoline era o amigo Da besta féra Nazista, Também se julgava um Deus Este fanfarrão fascista Mas este os aliados, Já o tinham posto na lista.

So the fact is there were six days	Eis que faltavam 6 dias
Until Berlin would be conquered,	P'ra Berlim ser conquistada,
When the news came	Quando veio uma noticia
A very happy and awaited bit of news	Feliz e muito esperada
The life of Mussolini	A vida de Mussoline
Had come to its end.	Tinha sido consumida.
He was killed by the citizens	Foi morto pelo seu povo
Of the very land of his birth	Da própria terra natal
He had been hung in the streets	Fôra enforcado na rua
Like any common animal	Como qualquer animal
After this the corpse was burned	Depois disto foi queimado,
Fulfilling his fatal destiny.	Cumprindo a sina fatal.
And days after the death,	E dias depois da morte
Of that murderous beast,	Daquela féra homicida,
Another solemn bit of news,	Outra noticia solene,
Similar to the previous one,	Com a outra parecida
Announced that Hitler,	Anunciava que Hitler,
In Berlin had lost his life.	Em Berlim perdêra a vida.
The cadaver was found	Foi encontrado o cadaver
Of this miserable monster	Deste monstro desgraçado
All riddled with bullets	Todo varado de balas
Totally mangled	Totalmente estraçalhado
The only thing not found was his soul,	Só não acharam su'alma,
Beezelbub had taken it away.	Belzebú tinha levado.
And yesterday the 8th of May	E ontem 8 de Maio
The entire world filled with joy	O mundo inteiro vibrou,
When the sun of liberty	Quando o sol da liberdade
Came newly to be seen	Novamente clareou
Sad Germany surrendered,	Rendeu-se a triste Alemanha,
The great war was over.	A grande guerra acabou.
The bells on high tolled	Dobrava os sinos no alto
The bells of the divine	Dos campanários Divinos
The sirens blew	As sirenas apitavam
The people came forth with hymns	O povo entoava hynos
Singing "Hozana to God in the highest"	Cantando Hozanas a Deus,
For such a happy ending.	Por tão felizes destinos.

Mark J. Curran

Only one more bit of harmony is lacking	Só falta mais harmonia
To celebrate this glorious moment,	P'ra celebrar esta Gloria,
Because one of the Allies	Porque um dos Aliados
One of the greats of history	Um dos grandes da historia
Died a few days before	Morreu poucos dias antes
The victory was dedicated.	De consagrar-se a vitória.
It was President Roosevelt	Era o presidente Roosevelt
This great American	Este grande Americano
The focal point of hope	O centro das esperanças
For the well-being of all humans	Para o bem estar humano
It was he who determined the destiny	Foi quem traçou os destinos
Of the tyrannical enemy.	Do inimigo tirano.
He was the supreme banner	Foi a bandeira suprema
Of the cause of the Allies,	Da causa dos aliados,
He succumbed full of glory	Sucumbiu cheio de glories
His remains are praised	Seus restos vão laureados
With the crown of virtue,	Com a côroa da virtude,
And his triumphs achieved.	E os triumfos alcançados.
England as well	A Inglaterra também
Possesses a great defender	Possui grande defensor
It is Prime Minister Churchill	É o ministro Churchirl
A man of great valor	Homem de muito valor
With his perseverance,	Com sua perseverance,
He defeated the invader.	Derrotou o invasor.
This man is of great worth	Este homem vale muito
For his tenacity,	Por sua tenacidade,
He found himself alone in the battle	Se viu na luta sosinho
Against barbarity	Contra a barbaridade
But by persevering, he won,	Mais insistindo venceu,
Win the conquest of liberty.	Conquistou a liberdade.
Brazil also has a name	O Brasil também tem nome
In this world war,	Nesta Guerra mundial,
Mr. Getúlio Vargas	O sr. Getúlio Vargas
As national chief	Como chefe nacional
Of our great Brazil,	Do nosso grande Brasil,
Conquered the forces of evil.	Venceu as forças do mal.

Brazil entered the war	O Brasil entrou na Guerra
Not to brag of its deeds,	Não para contar façanha,
But in defense of rights	Em defeza do direito
It faced a hard campaign	Enfrentou dura campanha
And today our flag	E hoje nossa bandeira
Waves in Germany.	Já tremula na Alemanha.
Long live the Brazilian fatherland	Viva a patria Brazileira
Long live France and England	Viva a França e Inglaterra
Long live Russia and the Americas	Viva a Rússia e as Américas
Long live the end of the war	Viva o término da Guerra
Long live all the Allied Forces	Viva todos aliados
Who are alive on the earth.	Que estão vivos na terra.
Long live President Vargas	Viva o prezidente Vargas
Long live the government of the state,	Viva o governo do estado,
And the Minister of Justice	E o ministro da justiça
Who has put forth such a great effort	Que tanto tem se esforçado
Long live the Minister of War,	Viva o ministro da Guerra,
For the triumph won.	Pelo triumfo alcançado.
D – I offer my "hurrahs" to Truman	Dou o meu viva a Truman
E – And long live the great Stalin	E viva o grande Stalin
L – And great cheers I also give	Longos vivas também dou
A – To whoever remembers me	A quem lembrar-se de mim
R – Ruination is the fate of great Germany	Ruiu a grande Alemanha
M – Hitler died in the campaign	Morreu Hitler na campanha
E – And the war finally ended.	E a guerra teve fim.
END Recife, May 12, 1945	FIM Recife 12-5-1945
Price – one cruzeiro	Preço – 1 Cruzeiro

Back Cover:

"Exclusive distributor of the publications of João Martins de Athayde: Perfume Shop Minerva, Frei Miguelinho Street, No. 87, Natal, Rio Grande do Norte (State). Higino Aguiar Perfumist."

"Distribuidor exclusive das publicações de João Martins de Atayde: Perfumaria Minerva, Rua Frei Miguelinho, n.87, Natal, Rio Grande do Norte. Higino Aguiar. Perfumista."

Cover of the story-poem "The Debate of Lampião and an American Tourist" by Franklin MAXADO Nordestino

9.

"Debate between Lampião and an American Tourist"
"Debate de Lampião com a Turista Americana"
Franklin Maxado Nordestino

    This unorthodox cordelian poem unites the classic northeastern bandit [cangaceiro] with a very modern theme of late twentieth century in Brazil: international feminism. It does so employing irony which coincidentally recalls both the name and the stylistic trademark of the famous Brazilian novelist Joaquim Maria Machado de Assis, whom Franklin Maxado must have had in mind when he chose his own penname in story-poems beginning his career in "cordel" in the 1970s.

    The story-poem deals with change, problems, and the vicissitudes in life that the end of the twentieth and early twenty-first centuries brought to Brazil, among them, the change of role of both men and women in society. This poem must have been shocking to traditional cordelian readers of the Northeast because it is a poem very different from the rest of "cordel." We surmise it was less shocking to the public buying Maxado's poems on the streets of São Paulo, the burgeoning metropolis of nearly twenty million people in southeast Brazil. The reader has to admit the possibility of a very satiric reading of the exaggerated sense of machismo of the traditional northeasterner, as well as the slightly arrogant role of the most famous pioneer of North American feminism, Betty Freidan and her "Feminine Mystique." The non-Brazilian reader may meet, perhaps for the first time, through the narrative vehicle of Franklin Maxado, a spiritist character, that is, the spiritist medium in the poem that is at the same time the bandit Lampião. Maxado arranges Lampião's obviously impossible appearance in the poem with Betty Freidan in the late twentieth century by means of the character Romeo, Betty's tourist guide, who has been converted into the famous bandit.[119]

---

119 Most readers in the United States are slightly familiar with the séance, the vibrating table or objects on it, or the voices of long deceased friends or family

Maxado Nordestino, in his time of "cordel" in the 1970s, 1980s and early 1990s, was one of the most controversial of cordelian poets in Brazil, first of all, because he was a college graduate specializing in journalism and later on in law. He did not have the natural gift of flowing, extemporizing verse of many of the "traditional" cordelian poets of the time, and he often made mistakes in syllable count and rhyme ["quebrar a métrica"]. But that did not worry him, perhaps since one of his models was the iconoclastic Bahian cordelian poet of the 1940s to the 1960s, José Gomes, penname Cuíca de Santo Amaro, the "hell's mouth," mud raking cordelian poet of Salvador for years. Cuíca was a poet renowned for "murdering" the metrics but writing scintillating tales of local gossip and politics.[120] For Maxado, it is the MESSAGE and the satiric tone that count: irreverent, biting and street-wise in greater São Paulo. It is interesting to note that the poet was originally from the Northeast, from Feira de Santana, two hours outside Salvador, a town famous for one of the largest cattle markets in Brazil, and was a disciple of one of his cordelian heroes, Rodolfo Coelho Cavalcante. He followed the "modus-operandi" of Cuíca de Santo Amaro, not being an excellent poet, but being incredibly efficient as a popular reporter of the masses. Maxado, as they used to say in Brazil, "put on a show," [deu um show] when he declaimed and sold his poetry on the streets of São Paulo. He looked like a hippy of the times -- long hair, round granny glasses, leather hat, vest and sandals. Bohemian and shocking in appearance, he entertained his public for years, making them nearly fall down with laughter and often, perhaps in the same poem, steam with anger over the ridiculous state of social

that are "called" by the medium to the table. But very few are familiar with the extremely important and popular Brazilian version: Brazilian Kardecism, that is, Brazilian spiritism originated by the Frenchman Allan Kardec in mid-nineteenth century in France. Kardec based his spiritism first of all on the Bible, taking the healing power of Jesus Christ as a model for spiritist healers. But he added a basic tenant of Reincarnation and communication with the spirits of the dead via the spiritist "medium." So Romeo, in this story, simply a tour guide, is converted by Machado first of all into a medium and then into the real Lampião.

120 Cuíca was a contemporary of Rodolfo Coelho Cavalcante, conservative moralist of his times, and was the exact opposite side of the coin. He was the third in our "Bahian Trilogy," following books on famed novelist Jorge Amado, then Rodolfo Coelho Cavalcante, and now Cuíca. See "Cuíca de Santo Amaro: Poeta-Repórter da Bahia," Salvador: Fundação Jorge Amado, 1990.

or political affairs at the time in Brazil. There is one additional factor in this specific poem which needs be addressed: it is the only cordelian poem of the times that this author encountered that used, on purpose, a "pidgin English" as a poetic technique and "arm" or "weapon" to wound, satirize and defeat the great American feminist. It is parody on the grand scale.

One can speculate on the moment: was there a significant enough understanding of English by Maxado's public in São Paulo for them to "catch" the humor of it all? He sold poems, among other places, in the Plaza of the Republic on Sunday mornings, the "hippy" fair in central São Paulo. There were probably many English-speaking tourists about as well as sophisticated Brazilian students. Be that as it may, the poem stands. It should be noted, however, that in "cordel's" traditional Northeast -- Recife, Caruaru, Campina Grande, João Pessoa, or even Bahia -- the cordelian public did not know English in those times.

So we have a poem which really has little to do with actual deeds of the northeastern bandit, but employs the stereotypical figure of Lampião as a macho northeasterner. The story-poem in many ways becomes a portrait of customs toward the end of the twentieth century in Brazil.

We leave the reader to make the final decision. Is this poem a diatribe against the new feminism by virtue of Lampião's victory over Betty, or is it a tongue in cheek statement in opposition to the old ways? Either way, the poem is hilarious and one should read it picturing the hippy poet declaiming before an entertained crowd on the streets, wisecracking, guffawing and maybe upsetting the karma of some of his public.

"The Debate of Lampião with an American Tourist
Franklin Maxado Nordestino

The other day an American woman
Visited our Northeast
She started in Pernambuco
Researching in the ranching zone[121]
The homeland of Lampião
The macho type of Brazil
And of all his tough henchmen.

The tourist was a person called
Betty Freidan
She went there as a tourist
In the aforesaid region
She was over there by Petrolina[122]
And the feminist woman
Found herself in that famous city.

Finding herself on an excursion
She visited the local museum
She was indoctrinating other persons
With her atheistic principles
All at once a soul came down
Entering without knocking
In the [spiritist] medium called Romeo.

"Debate de Lampião com uma Turista Americana"
Franklin Maxado Nordestino

Outro dia uma Americana
Visitou nosso Nordeste
Se meteu em Pernambuco
Pesquisando pelo Agreste
A terra de Lampião
Do brasileiro machão
E de seus cabras da peste.

Ela era uma tal
De Bete Fride chamada
Foi ali como turista
Na região visitada
'Teve lá por Petrolina
Viu a mulher feminina
Numa cidade afamada.

Quando estava em excursão
Visitou o seu museu
Doutrinava outras pessoas
Com o seu princípio atéu
Aí baixou uma alma
Sem precisar bater palmas[123]
No médium que era Romeo.

---

121 In the 1960s, 1970s and 1980s American researchers were ubiquitous throughout Brazil, including the Northeast. Such people were both admired but also under suspicion: in a time of great feelings of Brazilian nationalism, the left in particular warned of American incursions and plots to "steal" Brazilian resources, even the Amazon! So perhaps Maxado includes Betty in the group.

122 Petrolina is a significant backlands city in Pernambuco along the famous São Francisco River, the river of North-South unity in Brazil.

123 The clapping of hands is a backlands custom still in evidence in this writer's years in the Northeast. Instead of knocking on a door, the visitor or guest would clap his or her hands outside the house or entry gate, and say "you there in the house," [ó de casa].

Romeo was a tour guide	Romeu era guia turístico
A small, wiry mixed blood[124]	Um caboclo bem franzino
But right away he stuck out his chest	Mas estufou logo os peitos
Like one of the big bad guys	Como um rapaz malino
Receiving that spirit	Recebendo ese espírito
Which was not a dream	Que não era onírico
But a proud northeasterner.	Mas orgulhoso nordestino.
Right away he gave two tongue lashings	Deu logo uns dois esporros
And said: I'm the one in charge here	E disse: aqui eu mando
And anyone who doesn't like it	E quem não me aceitar
Can get the hell out	Que vá logo se mandando
Because my men obey me	Porque cabras me obedecem
Those that don't, leave.	Os que não querem, desertem.
If not, I'll start the castrating.	Senão então vou capando.
Bete Fride protestou:	Betty Friedan protestou:
Shouting that this was "impossible"	Gritando que era "impóssibou"
But the medium let out a shout	Mas, o médium deu um grito
That raised the hair on everyone:	Que a todos arrepiou:
I'm Captain Lampião[125]	Sou Capitão Lampião
And I'm not afraid of any dyke	E não temo sapatão
And I don't owe her any favors.	Não devo nenhum favor.
At that point the Yankee Gringa	Aí a gringa ianque
Shut up so as to not get beaten up	Se calou pra não apanhar
She saw that the situation was	Viu que a parada era
Tense and really tough	Tensa e dura de lascar
She preferred closing her mouth	Preferiu calar a boca
Acting like a mute	Parecendo que era moca
And just remained listening.	E ficou só a escutar.
Lampião at that moment	Lampião então tomou
Took his turn to speak	A palavra no momento
He began his speech	Começou o seu discurso
Without any shyness	Sem nenhum acanhamento
Everyone was afraid	Todos estavm com medo
Of what he was going to say.	Daquele seu pensamento.

---

124 The mixed blood in question in the Northeast interior is part white, part Indian blood [caboclo].

125 The bandits took on the military titles like "captain" that were commonly used in the times by the local political bosses ["coronéis."]

-- That business of feminism
Is the art of all ugly women
Who can't get a macho man
To whip her into line
So she hooks up with another woman
And then does her thing
Spouting a foreign doctrine

-- With me those dykes
Really have no choice
They better do what I command
If not, I'll brand their faces
And I don't want any short hair
Cut right down to the nape of the neck.
No mini-skirts or gay clothes either.

-- No string biquinis or maillots
Nor tight pants either
Not too much makeup on her face
Or any low cut blouses
I just want a feminine woman
Who's not afraid of a real man
To keep her satisfied.

-- A woman for me is like
My Maria Bonita[126]
Who gets everything she wants
From me without any shouting.
Not like those demanding ugly women
Who seem so insolent
Like soldiers in a garret.

Maria Bonita gets
Everything she wants from me
With love and compliments
Knowing how to be a woman
So don't come on with your shouting
Because I'll kill you and fry you up
And eat you with a knife and fork.

-- Essa coisa de feminismo
É arte de mule feia
Que não arranja home macho
Para lhe meter a peia
Assim pega outra mulé
E então faz o que quer
Com uma doutrina alheia.

-- Comigo é que essas machonas
Não tem escolha ou vez
Tem de fazer o que mando
Senão, eu ferro na tez
Não quero cabelo curto
Cortado no cucuruto.
Minissaia ou trajes gueis.

-- Não quero tanga ou maiôs
E nem calça apertada
Muita pintura na cara
Ou a blusa decotada
Eu só quero a mulé feme
Que a nenhum macho teme
Para ficar saciada.

-- Mulé para mim é como
A minha Maria Bonita
Que consegue de mim tudo
Sem precisar fazer grita
Como as feias exigentes
Que parecem insolentes
Ou soldado na gurita.

Maria Bonita consegue
De mim tudo que quer
Com cariño e agrado
E sabendo ser mulé
Agora não vem com grito
Porque senão mato e frito
E como de faca e colher.

---

126 Maria Bonita in fact was Lampião's faithful consort. She was originally a shoemaker's wife; Lampião came along, liked what he saw, and ran off with her. The two remained together until the final moment, a fiery shootout on a ranch in Sergipe State, both dying riddled with police bullets. It reminds North Americans of the last scenes in the movie "Bonnie and Clyde."

-- The woman who is a real woman
Gets everything in the softness
Of the bed with her macho man
Without giving even a peep
She dominates without complaining
She suggests without shouting
She lights the candle.

-- She doesn't bring demands
Like an American woman
Who says she doesn't need
A really cool man
As though she were the greatest
Of all human beings, the best
That nature ever created.

-- These fads arriving here
Brought by television to Brazil
Are attacking families
And the authority of all the fathers
Turning us into a Gomorra
A big fucking whorehouse
That's the Brazil you see today.

If things go on this way
I'll send them all to hell
Shut off the booze
Do in the all the dykes
I'll choose only good women
Put all the ugly ones in canoes
And pack them out of here.

-- I wont' leave one of them
To end up without a hoe
I'll put them all to work
To keep the farm planted
Put an end to this feminism
And all consumerism too
Stuff that doesn't amount to anything.

-- A mulé que é mulé
Arranja tudo no macio
Da cama, com o seu macho
Sem precisar dar um pio
Domina, sem reivindicar
Sugestiona sem gritar
Buta fogo no pavio.

-- Não vem com as exigença
Como gringa Americana
Dizendo não precisar
De um homem bem bacana
Como se fosse a maior
E dos seres, o melhor
Que a natureza profana.

-- Essa onda tá chegando
Ao Brasil com a tevê
Está atacando a família
E de todo pai, o poder
Nos tornando uma Gomorra
Um grande bordel da porra
É o Brasil que se vê.

Se continuar assim
Eu mando tudo pra zona
Canalizar a cachaça[127]
Acabar com as machona
Escolher as mulés boas
Butar as feias nas canoas
E não deixar virem a tona.

-- Não deixar uma cafona
Ficar sem uma enxada
Mandar todas trabalhar
Deixar a roça plantada
Acabar com o feminisimo
E com todo consumismo
Negócios que no dao nada.

---

[127] We translated the word "cachaça" to "booze" in this context. "Cachaça" is the national Brazilian drink, sugar cane rum, drunk straight by the outlanders who read "cordel," but popular in most of Brazil for middle and upper class folks in a drink with lime juice, sugar and lots of ice, a Brazilian "margarita."

-- As to the shameless woman
With me it's the club
With the devil my guarantee
They'll all get a beating
And if they don't cooperate
I'll beat the hell out of them
That's my take on it.

Bete Freidan hearing this
Reacted like a macho brute
She shouted to him that the rights
Of a woman are not only to mourn
Not just a matter of being a widow
Not just having nice curves
But a right to have rights.

-- Mister, you are an ignoramus
And a chauvinist pig
Who doesn't understand anyone
Much less, a feminist
You're one of the old time machos
Who are enemies of women
Doesn't know how to carry out a seduction.

-- If I'm a pig, you're an old sow
And one of the old white ones
That only has rancid bacon
Give me some respect, woman
I don't know if you're a macho
And I don't want to look down there
Since I suspect you might not be.

Then Lampião really got mad
He got freaking furious
He whipped off his big belt
And was more upset than ever
He grabbed Betty Freidan
Lit into her like the Cisco Kid[128]
When he was attacked.

-- Pois a mulher descarada
Comigo é no cacete
Como o Cão me garantindo
Buto tudo no porrete
E quem não quiser entrar
Eu vou butar pra lascar
Pois este é meu cacoete.

Bete Fride ouvindo isto
Deu uma de macho bruto
Gritou-lhe que os direitos
Da mulher não é só luto
Não é coisa de viúvas
Não é so ter belas curves
Mas direito resoluto.

-- O mister é um ignorante
É um porco chauvinista
Que não entende de gente
Quanto mais de feminista
É um dos machões antigos
Que da mulher são inimigos
Não sabe fazer conquista.

-- Se sou porco, tu é porca
E dessas brancas baé
Que dá um toucinho rançoso
Me arrespeite, sua mule
Que não sei se é um macho
E não quero olhar embaixo
Pois desconfio que não é.

Aí Lampião zangou-se
Esbravejou arretado
Tirou logo o currião
E ficou bem transtornado
Agarrou a Bete Fride
E deu uma de Cisco Kide
Quando estava afrontado.

---

[128] The young reader may have to ask Dad or Granddad about the Cisco Kid; he was an old time B western movie star from the days of black and white cinema. His main weapon was a bull whip.

He said beating a woman	Disse que bater em fêmea
Is ugly, but it was much worse	É feio, porém que era
Getting beat up by her	Bem pior apanhar dela
And that one was like a wild animal	E aquela era uma fera
Like a poisonous snake	Como cobra venenosa
Like an arrogant tyrant	Como tirana orgulhosa
Who seemed to be a witch.	Que parecia feiticeira.
And he laid the leather to her	E mandou o couro adentro
The gringa began to shout:	A gringa então gritava:
-- Oh my darling, wonderful	-- Oh! Mai darling, únderful
(And the more he hit her):	(E quanto mais apanhava):
-- Very good, very much	-- Véri gude, véri mátixe
Thank you, you really hit the spot	Sânquio, iou me dide xeque-mate[129]
She didn't know what she was saying.	Não sabia o que falava.
-- I've finally found my man	-- Agora eu achei mai men
No longer will I walk shouting	Vou largar de andar gritando
Through the streets of the States	Por estrites dos Esteites
And taking off my brassiere	E sutiãns tirando
I accept you like a thousand	Te aceito até como mil
Other women in Brrrazil	Outras fêmeas do Brrrasil
I'm going to protest no longer.	Não vou ficar protestando.
I'm going to go back into the kitchen	-- Eu vou é para a cozinha
To fry up your meat	Assar a sua carninha
Make your milk pudding	Fazer seu pirão de leite
Along with your piece of fat	Junto a uma gordurinha
I'm going to be just a simple housewife	Vou ser é dona de casa
Never again wanting to sprout wings	Nunca mais eu quero asas
Or speak of such divisive things.	Para falar dessa rinha.
I've learned my lesson well	Aprendi bem a lesson
A woman's place is in bed	Lugar de uoman é na cama
In the kitchen and the dining room	Na quitichen e na copa
And not out looking for fame	E não procurar a fama
And knowing how to be a woman	Saber muito ser mulher
Not ending up like just any old bag	Não ficar como uma qualquer
An old maid in disgrace.	Na solterice da disgrama.

---

129 The whole suggestion of sado-machism adds insult to injury on poor Betty Freidan.

Mark J. Curran

After that conversation	Depois dessa conversação
Lampião said, "tsk, tsk, tsk."	Lampião deu um muxoxo
Put his belt back on	Recolocou o cinturão
His waist and tightened it up	Na cintura e deu arrocho
Waved to everyone present	Saudou a todos presentes
And smiled between his teeth	Sorriu assim entre os dentes
And nodded his head.	Baixou a cabeça, mocho.
Before taking his leave	Antes de pedir licença
To climb back up to the stars	Para subir pro astral
Lampião had one word of warning:	Lampião deu um aviso:
For the woman who doesn't play it cool	A mulé que não fôr legal
Or doesn't get some common sense	Ou que não tomar juízo
I'll come back if necessary	Eu volto se fôr preciso
To have another little talk.	Fazendo outro falapau.
Then after that scandal	E após aquele escândalo
Lampião left his guide	Retirou-se do seu guia
All present said a quick prayer	Todos fizeram oração
Even Betty Freidan prayed	Até Bete Fride rezou
Romeo returned to himself	Romeu a si retornou
And nothing more was said.	Não teve mais falação.
F -- all the talking was done	F -- alação que deu foi eu.
M – by Maxado – the strong poet	M -- axado o poeta forte
A – thinking about Lampião	A -- chando que Lampião
X -- like he was there up North	X -- uxa como lá no Norte
A – perhaps times have changed	A -- caso os tempos mudaram
D -- from the night they invented	D -- e uma noite que inventaram
O -- such customs as these.	O -- s costumes desse porte.
End. São Paulo, October, 1981	Fim. São Paulo, outubro de 1981

Cover of the story-poem "Trip to São Saruê"
by Manoel Camilo dos Santos

10.

"Trip to St. Saruê"
"Viagem a São Saruê"
Manoel Camilo dos Santos

The final poem of this anthology is written in a style rare to "cordel" – it combines the narrative and the lyric modalities in a work that results in a true popular jewel of the medium. The author, Manoel Camilo dos Santos, some time deceased, was proud of his personal poetic gift, [dom da poesia] and his way with language, resulting in a nice turn of phrase in his poems. He owned his own small printing shop in Campina Grande, Paraíba State, and called it "The Star of Poetry," [Estrella da Poesia]. We interviewed him in 1966 in one of the poorest parts of Campina Grande. The poet met us at his front door, shirt and trousers heavily stained with the printing ink used in printing his "folhetos" and "romances." Manoel Camilo was also known in "cordel" as one of the most eloquent defenders of authors' rights. He defended the poets on the back covers [contra-capas] of his story-poems, excoriating in bombastic language, at times with sentiments bordering on paranoia, the offenders – thieves stealing other poets' works, including "indecent and unscrupulous poets" that he denounced publicly. Manoel Camilo announced to readers that his "team" of lawyers was standing ready to defend the rights of him and other poets.[130]

Orígenes Lessa, novelist and short story writer some time deceased, member of the prestigious Brazilian Academy of Letters in Rio de Janeiro, long-time fan and collector of "cordel," and finally, one of its most prominent patrons from the late 1950s to the 1980s, met the poet in the 1950s and interviewed him several times. For Lessa, Manoel Camilo's masterpiece is "St. Saruê," a poem which he says is a good example of Brazilian "escape" literature, popular as well as erudite, "a live portrait of flight, through the medium of the dream, of a people

---

[130] See Curran "A Página Editorial da Literatura de Cordel," <u>Revista Brasileira de Folclore</u>, v. 32, 5-16, jan.-abr. 1972.

who suffer."[131] He sees the poem as a backlands' version of the famous "I'm leaving for Passárgada" ["Vou – me embora p'ra Passárgada"] by the Modernist Manuel Bandeira, an icon of Brazilian erudite poetry.

The strange thing is that the poet himself considered the poem to be nothing more than "a common story-poem that I easily wrote -- a little poem of little effort."[132] According to Manoel Camilo dos Santos, the title was born of a saying or common popular phrase which, translated, is "Only in St. Saruê where the beans come up without rain," ["Só em São Saruê onde brota o feijão sem chuva"].[133] St. Saruê is thus "the improbable, the Day of St. Never, a silly little thing that the masses find humorous."[134] So the poet gave little importance to the poem and believed he had created much greater story-poems. Aforesaid writer Orígenes Lessa recited fragments of the poem in a convention of the Association of Brazilian Writers in Salvador in 1955, and consequently, the Brazilian erudite world came to know something of Northeastern folk-popular poetry. The poem was praised by no less that Manuel Bandeira and later by the icon of Brazilian letters, Carlos Drummond de Andrade.

According to another scholar of "cordel," Veríssimo de Melo, the two writers, Manoel Camilo dos Santos and the poet of the Brazilian Academy of Letters Manuel Bandeira, wanted to flee from reality and describe a land of happiness. For Bandeira happiness is found in an ideal country where the poet is a friend of the king and has everything he desires. For the humble folk-popular poet Manoel Camilo dos Santos happiness is found in a land where all are rich and do not need to work and there is no lack of basic food to live.[135] A curious thing is that the folk-popular version is in itself more lyrical that the well-known version by Bandeira.

---

131 Orígenes Lessa, <u>Anhembi</u>, 61, dez., 1955, p. 83.
132 Cited in <u>A Voz dos Poetas</u> ["The Voice of the Poets"] by Orígenes Lessa (Rio de Janeiro: Fundação Casa de Rui Barbosa, 1984), p. 59.
133 ibid.
134 Lessa, <u>A Voz dos Poetas</u>, p. 70.
135 <u>Cantador de Viola</u> [Poet-Singer of the "Guitar"] (Recife: Coleção Concórdia, 1961), p. 27.

The story-poem in itself created significant interest on the part of Brazilian intellectuals in "cordel," perhaps inaccurately, because the great majority of cordelian poems are not lyrical but narrative in tone. Nonetheless, this is a beautiful lyrical poem of great value especially in the sense of its folk-popular vision and the language it employs. Thus we choose "St. Saruê" to end the anthology. Manoel Camilo was, ironically, a master of the "romance," the long, narrative poem, a mainstay of "cordel." Such poems were epic pieces of love, suffering and the vanquishing of evil so common in "cordel," but it was this singular poem, "Trip to St. Saruê," that marked the poet in the annals of Brazilian popular poetry. If such a vision could come true, the sufferings of poor Northeasterners would be ameliorated. So far, no mortal messiah has saved them from poverty and hunger; this poem expresses the dream.

"Trip to St. Saruê"
Manoel Camilo dos Santos

"Viagem a São Saruê"
Manoel Camilo dos Santos

Dr. Master of Thought
Said to me one day: You,
Camilo, go visit
The country of St. Saruê
Since it's the best place
That you can see in this world.

Doutro Mestre Pensamento
Me disse um dia: Você
Camilo, vá visitar
O País São Saruê
Pois é o lugar melhor
Que neste mundo se vê.

Since I was little
I had always heard about
This place St. Saruê
It was my destiny to travel
By order of Master Thought
So I went to see the place.

Eu que desde pequeno
Sempre ouvia falar
Neste tal São Saruê
Destinei-me a viajar
Com ordem do pensamento
Fui conhecer o lugar.

I began the journey
At four o'clock in the morning
I took the coach of the breeze
I passed by the dawn
And next to the edge of the sea
I saw the astonishing sunrise.

Iniciei a viagem
As quatro da madrugada
Tomei o carro da brisa
Passei pela alvorada
Junto do quebrar da barra
Eu vi a aurora abismada.

Through the early morning mist	Pela aragem matutina
I sighted directly in front of me	Eu avistei bem defronte
The sister of the lovely dawn	A irmã da linda aurora
Who was bathing in a fountain	Que se banhava na fonte
And the sun now radiating	Já o sol vinha espargindo
From beyond the horizon.	No além do horizonte.
The day came forth in a smile	Surgiu o dia risonho
In imposing springtime	Na primavera imponente
The hours passed slowly	As horas passavam lentas
Space was incandescent	O espaço encandescente
The tame breeze transforming itself	Transformava a brisa mansa
Into a painful calm.	Em um mormaço dolente.
I switched from the coach of the breeze	Passei do carro da brisa
To the coach of the muggy stillness	Para o carro do mormaço
Which penetrated rapidly	O qual veloz penetrou
Far beyond in great space	No além do grande espaço
At the confines of the horizon	Nos confins do horizonte
I felt the tiredness of the day.	Sento do dia o cansaço.
As evening came on	Enquanto a tarde caía
Between mystery and secrets	Entre mistério e segredos
A gentle breeze docilely	A viração docilmente
Caressed the trees	Afagava os arvoredos
The final rays of the sun	Os últimos raios de sol
Bordered the tall rocks.	Bordavam os altos penedos.
The afternoon died and the night	Morreu a tarde e a noite
Assumed its leadership	Assumiu sua chefia
I left the calm and I switched	Deixei o mormaço e passei
To the coach of cold snow	Pro carro da neve fria
I saw the mysteries of the night	Vi os mistérios da noite
Awaiting the day.	Esperando pelo dia.
Upon the surging of the new dawn	Ao surgir da nova aurora
I felt the coach stop	Senti o carro parar
I looked and I saw a beach	Olhei e vi uma praia
Sublime in its enchantment	Sublime de encantar
A rough sea bathing	O mar revolto banhando
The dunes at the edge of the water.	As dunas da beira-mar.

Bibliography of Secondary Works on "Cordel"

Since most of these sources are printed in Portuguese, we leave the entry in that language; there are but a few titles in English and we present them as such.

Almeida, A. e Sobrinho, José Alves. <u>Marcos 1</u>. Romanceiro Popular Nordestino. Campina Grande: MEC, EDITEL, 1981.

Amâncio, Geraldo e Pereira, Vanderley. <u>De Repente Cantoria</u>. Fortaleza: LCR, 1995.

Andrade, Mário de. <u>Ensaio sobre a Música Brasileira</u>. São Paulo: Livraria Martins, 1962.

Angelo, Assis. <u>Presença dos Cordelistas e Cantadores Repentistas em São Paulo</u>. São Paulo: Instituição Brasileira de Difusão Cultural Ltda., 1996.

<u>Autores de Cordel</u>. Ed. Marlyse Meyer. São Paulo: Abril Editora, 1980.

Azevedo, Téo. <u>Cantador Verso e Viola</u>. 2a. ed. São Paulo: Letras e Letras, n.d.

Azevedo, Téo. Repente Folclore. Belo Horizonte: SESC, n.d.

Barroso, Gustavo. Ao Som da Viola. Rio de Janeiro: Dep. de Imprensa Nacional, 1949.

Barroso, Gustavo. Terra do Sol. Rio de Janeiro: Livraria José Olympio, 1956.

Batista, Sebastião Nunes. Antologia da Literatura de Cordel. Natal: Fundação José Augusto, 1977.

Batista, Sebastião Nunes. Bibliografia Prévia de Leandro Gomes de Barros. Rio de Janeiro: Biblioteca Nacional, 1971.

Batista, Sebastião Nunes. Poética Popular do Nordeste. Estudos, Nova Série. Rio de Janeiro: FCRB, 1982.

Bradesco-Goudemand, Yvonne. O Ciclo dos Animais na Literatura Popular do Nordeste. Estudos, Nova Série. Rio de Janeiro: FCRB, 1982.

Brasil/Brazil. n. 14, ano 8. 1995. cf. Mark J. Curran, "Grande Sertão: Veredas' e a Literatura de Cordel."

Caderno de Letras, Número Especial de Literatura Popular. João Pessoa: UFPB. n.3. ano2. julho/1978.

Calasans, José. Canudos na Literatura de Cordel. Ensaios 110. São Paulo: Atica, 1984.

Câmara Cascudo, Luís da. Cinco Livros do Povo. Rio: José Olympio, 1953.

Câmara Cascudo, Luís da. Flor dos Romances Trágicos. Rio de Janeiro: Editora do Autor, 1966.

Câmara Cascudo, Luís da. Vaqueiros e Cantadores. 2a. ed. Rio de Janeiro: Edições de Ouro, 1968.

Camargo, Nara Pereira de. "Usos da Forma da Literatura de Cordel". IN: Uma Questão Editorial. ano.1. n. 1. São Paulo, 23 de junho de 1978.

Campos, Eduardo. Folclore do Nordeste. Rio de Janeiro: Edições O Cruzeiro, 1959.

Carneiro Campos, Renato. Ideologia dos Poetas Populares. Recife: MEC-INEP-Centro de Pesquisas Educacionais do Recife, 1959.

Carvalho, Gilmar de. Publicidade em Cordel o Mote do Consumo. Rio de Janeiro: Fundação Waldemar Alcântara, n.d.

Carvalho, Rodrigues de. Cancioneiro do Norte. 3rd. ed. Rio de Janeiro: MEC-INL, 1967.

Cordel (O) e os Desmantelos do Mundo. Antologia, Nova Série. Rio de Janeiro: FCRB, 1983.

Cordel (O) no Grande Rio. Catálogo. Rio de Janeiro: INEPAC, Divisão de Folclore, 1985.

Cordel (O) Testemunha da História do Brasil. Antologia, Nova Série. Rio de Janeiro: FCRB,1987.

Coutinho Filho, F. Violas e Repentes. Recife: Saraiva, 1953.

Cuíca de Santo Amaro. Introdução. Mark J. Curran. São Paulo: Hedra, 2000.

Curran, Mark J. Cuíca de Santo Amaro Poeta - Repórter da Bahia. Fundação Casa de Jorge Amado, 1990.

Curran, Mark J. "Grande Sertão: Veredas na Literatura de Cordel". IN: Brasil/Brazil. Ano 8. N. 14, 1995.

Curran, Mark J. História do Brasil em Cordel. São Paulo: EDUSPE, 1998.

Curran, Mark J. <u>Jorge Amado na Literatura de Cordel</u>. Salvador da Bahia: Fundação Cultural do Estado da Bahia – Fundação Casa de Rui Barbosa, 1980.

Curran, Mark J. <u>La Literatura de Cordel Brasileña: Antología Bilingüe</u>. Madrid: Editorial Orígenes, 1991.

Curran, Mark J. <u>(A) Literatura de Cordel</u>. Recife: Universidade Federal de Pernambuco, 1973.

Curran, Mark J. <u>(A) Presença de Rodolfo Coelho Cavalcante na Moderna Literatura de Cordel</u>. Rio de Janeiro: Nova Fronteira-Fundação Casa de Rui Barbosa, 1987.

Daus, Ronald. <u>O Ciclo Epico dos Cangaceiros na Poesia Popular do Nordeste</u>. Estudos, Nova Série. Rio de Janeiro: FCRB, 1982.

Diégues Júnior, Manuel. 2a. ed. <u>Literatura de cordel</u>. Rio de Janeiro:MEC-FUNARTE, 1975.

Ferreira, Jerusa Pires. <u>Armadilhas da Memória (Conto e Poesia Popular)</u>. Salvador: Fundação Casa de Jorge Amado, 1991.

Ferreira, Jerusa Pires. <u>Cavalaria em Cordel</u>. São Paulo: Hucitec, 1979.

Ferreira, Jerusa Pires. <u>Fausto no Horizonte</u>. São Paulo: Hucitec, 1992.

<u>João Martins de Atayde</u>. Introdução. Mário Souto Maior. São Paulo: Hedra, 2000.

Laurentino, José. <u>Poesia do Sertão</u>. Olinda: Casa das Crianças de Olinda, 1996.

Lessa, Orígenes. <u>Getúlio Vargas na Literatura de Cordel</u>. Rio de Janeiro: Editora Documentário, 1973.

Lessa, Orígenes. Inácio da Catingueira e Luís Gama, Dois Poetas Negros contam o Racismo dos Mestiços. Estudos. Nova Série. Rio de Janeiro: FCRB, 1982.

Lessa, Orígenes. (A) Voz dos Poetas. Estudos, Nova Série. Rio de Janeiro: FCRB,1984.

Literatura de Cordel. Antologia. Fortaleza: Banco do Nordeste, 1982.

Literatura Popular em Verso. Vol. 1. Antología. Rio de Janeiro: MEC-CRB, 1964.

Literatura Popular em Verso. Vol. 1. Catálogo. Rio de Janeiro: MEC-CRB, 1961.

Literatura Popular em Verso. Vol. 1. Estudos. Rio de Janeiro: MEC-FCRB, 1973.

Literatura Popular em Verso. Vol. 2. Antologia. Leandro Gomes de Barros -1. Rio de Janeiro: MEC-FCRB-Universidade Regional do Norte, 1976.

Literatura Popular em Verso. Vol. 3. Antologia. Leandro Gomes de Barros - 2. Rio de Janeiro: MEC-FCRB-UFEPB, 1977.

Literatura Popular em Verso. Vol. 4. Antologia. Francisco das Chagas Batista. Rio de Janeiro – MEC-FCRB, 1977.

Literatura Popular em Verso. vol. 5. Antologia. Leandro Gomes de Barros - 3. Rio de Janeiro: MEC-FCRB-UFPB, 1980.

Literatura Popular Portuguesa. Lisboa: Fundação Calouste Gulbenkian, 1992.

Londres, Maria José F. Cordel do Encantamento às Histórias de Luta. São Paulo: Livraria Duas Cidades, 1983.

Lopes, Antônio. Presença do Romanceiro. Rio de Janeiro: Edta. Civilização Brasileira, 1967.

Lunário Prognóstico Perpétuo. Jeronymo Cortez, Valenciano. Porto: Lello e Irmão, n.d. Cópia xerocada.

Luyten, Joseph. Bibliografia Especializada sobre Literatura Popular em Verso. São Paulo: Edta. Comunicações e Artes, 1981.

Luyten, Joseph Maria. (A) Literatura de Cordel em São Paulo Saudosismo e Agressividade. São Paulo: Edições Loyola, 1981.

Luyten, Joseph M. "Literatura de Cordel: Tradição e Atualidade" IN: Uma Questão Editorial . Ano. 2. N. 2. Sáó Paulo: 27 dezembro de 1979.

Luyten, Josph M. (A) Notícia na Literatura de Cordel. São Paulo: Escola de Comunicações e Artes, tese, 1984.

Luyten, Joseph M. O Que É Literatura Popular. São Paulo: Editora Brasiliense, 1983.

Luyten, Joseph M. Organizador. Um Século de Literatura de Cordel, Bibliografia Especializada. São Paulo: Nosso Studio Gráfico, Ltda., 2001.

Manoel Caboclo. Introduçáó. Gilmar de Carvalho. São Paulo: Hedra, 2000.

Maranhão de Souza, Liedo. Classificação Popular da Literatura de Cordel. Petrópolis: Edta. Vozes, 1976.

Maranhão de Souza, Liedo. (O) Folheto Popular, Sua Capa e Seus Ilustradores. Recife: Fundação Joquim Nabuco-Editora Massangana, 1981.

I then sighted a city	Avistei uma cidade
Like none I had ever seen	Como nunca vi igual
All covered with gold	Toda coberta de ouro
And encrusted with crystal	E forrada de crystal
No poor person exists there	Ali não existe pobre
Everything in general is rich.	É tudo rico em geral.
A bar of pure gold	Uma barra de ouro puro
Served as a placard I saw	Servindo de placa eu vi
With its letters formed in diamonds	Com as letras de brilhante
Arriving closer I read	Chegando mais perto eu li
It said: St. Saruê	Dizia: São Saruê
Is this place here.	É este lugar aqui.
When I saw its people	Quando avistei o povo
I was totally astonished	Fiquei de tudo abismado
A happy and strong people	Uma gente alegre e forte
A civilized people	Um povo civilizado
Good, easy to deal with, well-doing	Bom, tratável e benfazejo
And I was embraced by them all.	Por todos fui abraçado.
The people in St. Saruê	O povo em São Saruê
All possess happiness	Tudo tem felicidade
They live well, they dress well	Passa bem, anda decente.
And there is no contrariness	Não há contrariedade
One does not need to work	Não precisa trabalhar
And there is money to burn.	E tem dinheiro a vontade.
There the bricks of the houses	Lá os tijolos das casas
Are of crystal and marble	São de cristal e marfim
The doors are sheets of silver	As portas barras de prata
And door latches of ruby	Fechaduras de "rubim"
The roof tiles sheets of gold	As telhas folhas de ouro
And the floors of satin.	E o piso de cetim.
There I saw rivers of milk[136]	Lá vi rios de leite
Stacks of roasted beef	Barreiras de carne assada
Lakes of honey from bees	Lagoas de mel de abelha
And bogs of buttermilk	Atoleiros de coalhada
Ponds filled with Port wine	Açudes de vinho do porto.
And mounds of stewed meat.	Montes de carne guisada.

---

136 In the following strophes follows a list of northeastern foodstuffs, some with names which are often regional and not really translatable to English. We leave in these cases the text in its original Portuguese, at times with Indigenous names, and indicate the sense of the words in footnotes.

The stones in St. Saruê	As pedras de São Saruê
Are of cheese and rock candy sugar[137]	São de queijo e rapadura
The wells there are full of coffee	As cacimbas são café
Already made and hot	Já coado e com quentura
And beyond all this	De tudo assim por diante
Everything exists in great plenty.	Existe grande fartura.
Beans there come up in the field	Feijão lá nasce no mato
Ready and already cooked	Maduro e já cozinhado
Rice comes up in the lowlands	O arroz nasce nas várzeas
Hulled and ready to eat	Já prontinho e dispolpado
Turkeys are born already brushed	Perú nasce de escôva
They live satisfied without eating.	Sem comer vive cevado.
Hens lay eggs every day	Galinha põe todo dia
But instead of eggs, capons	Invés de ovos é capão
And wheat instead of grains	O trigo invés de semente
Produces loaves of bread	Bota cachadas de pão
Butter there falls from the clouds	Manteiga lá cai das nuvens
Piling up on the ground.	Fazendo ruma no chão.
The fish there are so tame	Os peixes lá são tão mansos
Accustomed as they are to people	Como o povo acostumados
They leave the sea, come to the house	Saem do mar vêm pras casas
They are big, fat and well fed	São grandes, gordos e cevados
Just a matter of picking them up and eating	É só pegar e comer
Since they all live already stewed.	Pois todos vivem guisados.

---

137 The Portuguese "rapadura" is a typical food of all the North of Brazil, a product always present in the local fair or regional market, a food that the northeasterner consumes as a general sweet and at times as a "dessert" with coffee. The name, as folklorist Luís da Câmara Cascudo informs, comes from the fact that it is hardened sugar and one has to scrape it with a sharp knife to eat. It is the "açúcar panela" of Cuba or Panamá. The old northeastern sugar mills still produce "rapadura," as we witnessed on a trip to the sugar plantations of the family of José Lins do Rego, famous writer of the "Generation of 1930," nationally recognized for his important novels of the "Sugar Cane Cycle" in the 1940s and 1950s, among them "Plantation Boy" ["Menino de Engenho"] and "Dead Fire" ["Fogo Morto"], the latter referring to the mill whose production has ceased.

Everything there is good and easy	Tudo lá é bom e fácil
You don't need to buy anything	Não precisa se comprar
There is no hunger or sickness	Não há fome nem doença
Folks live to enjoy themselves	O povo vive a gozar
They have everything and nothing is lacking	Tem tudo e não falta nada
And there's no need to work.	Sem precisar trabalhar.
They don't plant "maniva"[138] there	Maniva lá não se planta
It grows instead of manioc[139]	Nasce em vez de mandioca
It sprouts loaves of manioc bread[140]	Bota cachos de beijú
And handfuls of tapioca	E palmas de tapioca
Corn on the cob is already "pamonha"[141]	Milho a espiga é pamonha
And the corn is popcorn.	E o pindão é pipoca.
Sugar cane in St. Saruê	A cana em São Saruê
Has no waste parts (funny!)	Não tem bagaço (é gozado)
Some stalks are filled with honey	Umas são canos de mel
Others with refined sugar	Outras açúcar refinado
The leaves are made into belts	As folhas são cinturão
Like kid leather, well tanned.	De pelica e bem chomado.

---

138 The entire strophe consists in food names, most of them of Indigenous origin. The word "Mani" is the name of a Tupi Indian princess, and together with the ending "oca," meaning "the house of," it forms the complete word "mandioca" or manioc in English. We surmise that "maniva" is a variation of manioc.

139 "Mandioca" is "casaba" in the Spanish Caribbean. It is one of the native foods of Brazil, a staple among the Indians. But one must distinguish between "wild manioc" ["mandioca braba"] from which the common manioc flour is derived, and "sweet manioc" ["mandioca doce" or "aipim"], the sweet root the Indians eat roasted over fire and from which they made their famous alcoholic drink, "cauim." The latter has a very folkloric preparation: the root is chewed, the liquid spat out into a container and later fermented. Manioc flour is still eaten in Brazil, ever present on the food table in the Northeast; it is eaten with beans and rice, and even alone, "popped into the mouth" like popcorn by the poor.

140 Manioc bread or "beiju" is another Indian food, resembling a thin pancake made of manioc flour, a sort of "Indian bread."

141 "Pamonha" is also a food of Indian origin; it is a sort of small bread or even like a pie crust made of the flour of green corn with cinnamon, cooked in water and salt, wrapped in banana leaves. In Brazilian erudite literature, the novelist Jorge Amado describes all these foods as "typical foods" of the June festivals of the Northeast, most prominently in "Tereza Batista, Tired of War," ["Tereza Batista Cansada de Guerra"].

Mark J. Curran

There are trees there of cashmere	Lá os pés de casimira
Denim, rubber and tropicals	Brim borracha e tropical
There's nycron, "beiga" and linen	De nycron, beiga e linho
And the famous "diagonal"	E o famoso diagonal
They produce clothing ready to wear	Já bota as roupas prontas
Perfectly fitting the people.	Próprias para o pessoal.
The trees of hats for everyone	Os pés de chapéu de massa
Are all large and full	São tão grandes e carregados
Those with stylish shoes	Os de sapatos de moda
Each cluster of branches is overloaded	Têm cada cachos "aloprados"
The trees with silk stockings	Os pés de meias de seda
Wow, they live "bursting at the seams."	Chega vivem "escangalhados."
There are farms with money trees	Sítios de pés de dinheiro
That really get your attention	Que faz chamar atenção
The branches with the large notes	Os cachos de notas grandes
Man, they are dragging on the ground	Chega arrastram pelo chão
The silver and gold bushes	As moitas de prata e ouro
Are thick as cotton.	São mesmo que algodão.
The trees with thousand dollar notes	Os pés de notas de mil
Covering them like a cape	Carrega chega encapota
You can pick all you want	Pode tirar-se a vontade
The more you pick the more they grow.	Quanto mais tira mais bota
Aside from the bunches they have	Além dos cachos que tem
Shells or leaves, everything is money.	Casca e folha tudo é nota.
There when a child is born	Lá quando nasce um menino
It's no trouble to raise him	Não dá trabalho a criar
He's already talking and knows how	Já é falando e já sabe
To read, write and count	Ler, escrever e contar
He jumps, runs, sings and does	Salta, corre, canta e faz
Everything commanded of him.	Tudo quanto se mandar.
There you don't see any homely women	Lá não se ver mulher feia
They are all young and beautiful	É toda moça e formosa
Well educated and brought up	Bem educada e decente
Well dressed and friendly	Bem trajada e amistosa
It's like a garden of fairies	É qual um jardim de fadas
Replete with carnations and roses.	Repleto de cravo e rosa.

There they have a river called	Lá tem um rio chamado
The fountain of youth	O banho da mocidade
In which an old man of one hundred years	Onde um velho de cem anos
Bathing whenever he wants	Tomando banho a vontade
When he leaves the water he appears	Quando sai fora parece
To be twenty years old.	Ter vinte anos de idade.
It's a magnificent place	É um lugar magnífico
Where I spent many days	Onde eu passei muitos dias
Well satisfied and taking	Bem satisfeito e gozando
My pleasure in good health and happiness	Prazer, saúde e alegrias
And all that time I occupied myself	Todo esse tempo ocupei-me
In reciting poetry.[142]	Em recitar poesias.
There exists everything that is beautiful[143]	Lá existe tudo quando é de beleza
Everything that is good and pretty	Tudo quanto é bom, belo e bonito
It seems a holy and blessed place	Parece um lugar santo e bandito
Or a garden of divine nature	Ou jardim da divina Natureza
It imitates well in its grandeur	Imita muito bem pela grandeza
The ancient promised land	A terra da antiga promissão
Where Moses and Aaron	Para onde Moisés e Aaraão
Led the people of Israel	Conduziam o povo de Israel
Where they say ran milk and honey	Onde dizem que corriam leite e mel
And manna from heaven fell to the earth.	E caía manjar do céu no chão.
Everything there is festive and in harmony	Tudo lá é festa e harmonia
Love, peace, good will and happiness	Amor, paz, benquer, felicidade
Rest, calm and friendship	Descanso, sossego e amizade
Pleasure, tranquility and joy	Prazer, tranqüilidade e alegria
On the eve of the day I left	Na véspera de eu sair naquele dia
I gave a speech in verse there	Um discurso poético lá eu fiz
And they gave me at the command of a judge	Me deram a mandado de um juiz
A ring of diamonds and rubies	Um anel de brilhante e de "rubim"
On which is written as follows:	No qual um letreiro diz assim:
-- He who visits this country is happy.	-- É feliz quem visita este País.

---

142 Manoel Camilo, like few others of his cordelian colleagues, at times launches himself into poetic heights (for example at the beginning of the poem) and is well aware of his role as poet, as a special person with a special gift of which is he is justly proud. This is an example of the "role of the poet" so discussed by the scholars of "cordel."

143 This strophe consists in ten lines of verse, the "décima" in cordelian parlance, a metric form much more common to the "poet-singer" [cantador] than the normal forms used in "cordel." In this case it is just one more example of the poetic talent that Manoel Camilo wants to display.

I shall finish with this advice	Vou terminar avisando
To any small friend	A qualquer amiguinho
Who perhaps should want to visit there	Que quiser ir para lá
I can show him the way	Posso ensinar o caminho
But I'll only show it to he	Porém só ensino a quem
Who buys a poem from me.[144]	Me comprar um folhetinho.
End.	Fim.

---

[144] Manoel Camilo closes his poem in the most traditional style, asking his public to buy his story in verse, a final strophe common to "cordel" and almost formulaic in style. It is interesting to note the poetic turn of phrase similar to the famous Spanish "romance," "Count Arnold" ["El Conde Arnaldos"] whose poet says at the end that "I will only show the way to he who goes with me."

Maranhão de Souza, Liedo. (O) Mercado, Sua Praça e a Cultura Popular do Nordeste. Recife: Prefeitura Municipal do Recife-Secretaria de Educação e Cultura, 1977.

Matos, Edilene. Ele o Tal Cuíca de Santo Amaro. 2a, ed. Salvador: Sec. da Cultura e Turismo do Estado da Bahia, 1998.

Matos, Edilene. (O) Imaginário da Literatura de Cordel. Salvador: UFBA, 1986.

Matos, Edilene. Notícia Biográfica do Poeta Popular Cuíca de Santo Amaro. Centro de Estudos Baianoa. Salvador: UFBA, 1985.

Maurício, Ivan; Cirano, Marcos; Almeida, Ricardo de. Arte Popular e Dominação. Recife: Editora Alternativa, 1978.

Maxado, Franklin, O Cordel Televivo. Rio de Janeiro: Códecri, 1984.

Maxado, Franklin. Cordel, Xilogravuras e Ilustrações. Rio de Janeiro: Edta. Códecri, 1984.

Maxado, Franklin. O Que E' Literatura de Cordel? Rio de Janeiro: Códecri, 1980.

Mota, Leonardo. Cantadores. 3rd. ed. Fortaleza, Imprensa Universitária do Ceará, n.d.

Mota, Leonardo. No Tempo de Lampião. Fortaleza: Imprensa Universitária do Ceará, 1967.

Mota, Leonardo. Sertão Alegre. Fortaleza: Imprenta Universitária do Ceará, 1965.

Mota, Leonardo. Violeiros do Norte. Fortaleza, UFCeará, n.d.

Patativa do Assaré. Introdução. Sylvie Debs. São Paulo: Hedra, 2000.

Peregrino, Umberto. Literatura de Cordel em Discussão. Rio de Janeiro: Presença, 1984.

Pereira da Costa, Francisco Augusto. Folklore Pernambucano. Rio de Janeiro: Livraria J. Leite, 1908.

Proença, Ivan Cavalcanti. A Ideologia do Cordel. 2a. ed. Rio de Janeiro: Editora Brasília, Rio, 1977.

Revista de Ciências Sociais. Número especial: cordel. Fortaleza: UFC. N. 1-2. V.VIII. 1977.

Revista do Departamento de Extensão de Cultura. Recife: DECA, ano IV, n. 6. 1962.

Revista do Departamento de Extensão de Cultura. Recife: DECA, ano VI, n.7, 1964.

Ribeiro, Lêda Tâmego. Mito e Poesia Popular. Prêmio Sílvio Romero. Rio de Janeiro:FUNARTE/Institutio Nacional do Livro, 1985.

Rodolfo Coelho Cavalcante. Introdução. Eno Wanke. São Paulo: Hedra, 2000.

Romero, Sílvio. Cantos Populares do Brasil. Vol. 1,2,3. Rio de Janeiro: Edta. José Olympio, 1954.

Romero, Sílvio. Estudos sobre a Poesia Popular do Brasil. 2a. ed. Petrópolis: Edta. Vozes, 1977.

Salles, Vicente. Repente e Cordel. Prêmio Sílvio Romero. Rio de Janeiro: FUNARTE, 1981.

Santos, Manoel Camilo dos. Autobigrafia do Poeta Manoel Camilo dos Santos. João Pessoa: Editora Universitária da UFEPB, 1979.

Saraiva, Arnaldo. Literatura Marginalizada. Porto: 1975.

Slater, Candace. Stories on a String, the Brazilian 'Literatura de Cordel'. Berkeley: U. of California, 1982.

Slater, Candace. (A) Vida no Barbante Rio de Janeiro: Civilização Brasileira, 1984.

Sobrinho, José Alves. Glosário da Poesia Popular. Campina Grande: EDITEL,1982.

Souza, Arlindo Pinto de. Editando o Editor. São Paulo: EDUSP,1995.

Tavares Júnior, Luíz. O Mito na Literatura de Cordel. Rio de Janeiro: Tempo Brasileiro, 1980.

Terra, Ruth Lêmos Brito. A Literatura de Folhetos nos Fundos Villa-Lobos. São Paulo: Instituto de Estudos Brasileirosda Universidade de São Paulo, 1981.

Wanke, Eno Teodoro. Vida e Luta do Trovador Rodolfo Coelho Cavalcante. Rio de Janeiro: Folha Carioca Editora Ltda., 1983.

Xilogravura (A) Popular e a Literatura de Cordel. Brochure. Rio de Janeiro: FCRB, 1985.

Zé Vicente. Introdução. Vicente Salles. São Paulo: Hedra, 2000.

CPSIA information can be obtained
at www.ICGtesting.com
Printed in the USA
BVHW071332010721
610862BV00008B/322